MANAGING THE RISKS OF

PAYMENT SYSTEMS

MANAGING THE RISKS OF
PAYMENT SYSTEMS

Paul S. Turner
Diane B. Wunnicke

WILEY

John Wiley & Sons, Inc.

658.155
T 95m

For general information on our other products and services, or technical support, please contact our Customer Care Department within the United States at 800-762-2974, outside the United States at 317-572-3993 or fax 317-572-4002.

Wiley also publishes its books in a variety of electronic formats. Some content that appears in print may not be available in electronic books.

For more information about Wiley products, visit our web site at www.wiley.com.

Library of Congress Cataloging-in-Publication Data:

Turner, Paul S.
Managing the risks of payment systems / Paul S. Turner, Diane B. Wunnicke.
    p. cm.
Includes bibliographical references.
  ISBN 0-471-32848-0 (Cloth)
1. Electronic funds transfer. 2. Payment. 3. Risk management. 4. Corporations—Finance. I. Wunnicke, Diane B. II. Title.
  HG1710.T87 2003
  658.15'5–dc21   2002156141

Printed in the United States of America

10 9 8 7 6 5 4 3 2 1

Contents

v

Contents

Contents

Contents

Contents

Contents

Contents

Preface

PAUL S. TURNER

I first became familiar with the risks of payment systems as a lawyer at Occidental Petroleum Corporation, advising the Occidental treasury department. I then became an advisor to the uniform law commissioners who wrote Article 4A (Funds Transfers) of the Uniform Commercial Code (U.C.C.) and revised U.C.C. Articles 3 (Negotiable Instruments), 4 (Bank Deposits and Collections), and 5 (Letters of Credit). More recently, I have served as a member of the Payments Advisory Group of the Association for Financial Professionals and as a Vice Chair of the American Bar Association's Payments Committee, a subcommittee of the Association's Business Law Section.

In all of these capacities, I have had the good fortune to form lasting and rewarding professional relationships with corporate treasury and bank executives, counsel to banks, and counsel to corporate customers. It has been interesting to observe that although knowledge and experience are fairly equally represented on both sides of the table in complex negotiations, the risks arising from mundane issues such as fraud, are, from a legal point of view, better understood by bankers and their counsel than by corporate treasury executives and their counsel.

Preface

It is my hope that this book, which is written for all interested parties, including bankers, corporate executives, and their respective counsel, will make the risks associated with the payment systems better understood by all.

DIANE B. WUNNICKE

As a veteran corporate finance manager, I came to know the risks of corporate payment systems. These systems and their risks were first introduced to me in the 1970s when I worked on the first on-line systems for a large savings and loan and its multiuser data processing service company. I came to understand the structure, requirements, and risks of banking payment systems as we installed our on-line customer systems, including single and multi-institution ATM machines and ACH payment processing. During the 1980s through the mid-1990s, I was finance and cash manager for a global energy company. We sought out every new cash management product that would help our domestic and international multicurrency payment operations. I arranged for our office to beta test new payment systems products and reporting. We all welcomed the Treasury Management Association and its successes for both corporate treasury departments and banks.

I hope that this book's practical explanations of the issues and management of corporate payment systems risks will be a helpful guide. Much longer books on specific topics and laws are available, and a lot of information is now timely updated and available on the Internet. (See References section.) I hope that the format of this book and its content provide the convenient, basic desk reference so often needed.

* * *

We both thank James Caldarella, former head of systems development for payment systems with a major global bank, for his insights into the risks of corporate payment systems and his perspectives as a highly experienced senior banker.

MANAGING THE
RISKS OF
PAYMENT
SYSTEMS

1

"We Didn't Know" Is No Excuse

This book is about the risks that business entities are likely to encounter in their use of the payment systems employed in the United States.

This chapter emphasizes that corporate managers who are responsible for the management of payment risks should understand how the law governing liability for fraudulent checks and funds transfers determines whether the company or the bank is liable for fraud losses and, in addition, should understand whether the wording of the company's agreements with its bank would make the company liable for a loss even though the law would otherwise make the bank liable for it.

Ignorance of the law is not an excuse for poor management of payment systems risks.

WHAT IS A PAYMENT SYSTEM?

By "payment," we mean generally the process by which a debtor discharges indebtedness to a creditor. Of course, a payment can

1

be used for family, charitable, or other strictly consumer purposes, but this book is about business uses. By "system," we mean an arrangement of national or international scope by which debts may be discharged. Payment systems typically also include the processes by which the payors and participating financial institutions settle with each other.

PAYMENT SYSTEMS

There are primarily three kinds of payment systems:

1. Payment in the national currency (e.g., U.S. dollar bills and coins),
2. Payment by check, and
3. Paperless payments.

The paperless payment is a relatively new device as compared with payment in currency and payment by check. Paperless payments today are typically made by electronic means, and payments made by electronic means are commonly referred to as "wire transfers." The electronic funds-transfer systems in the United States include:

- The Fedwire system of the Federal Reserve Banks
- **CHIPS (Clearing House Interbank Payment System)** of the New York Clearing House Association and participating banks
- **SWIFT (Society for Worldwide International Telecommunications)**
- The **ACH (automated clearing house)** system of the National Automated Clearing House Association, using the processing facilities of the Federal Reserve system.

The Fedwire system and CHIPS are called "wholesale" funds-transfer systems because they normally involve the business-to-business transfer of very large sums. SWIFT is an international message transmission system. SWIFT differs from the other systems described in this book in that it does not provide settlement services for its participants.

The ACH system is generally used for transfers in relatively lower amounts than are transferred in wholesale transfers. As these terms are generally used, ACH transfers, although electronic, are not called "wire" transfers. The ACH system is the only system described in this book that supports both credit and debit transfers. In an ACH credit transfer, the *payor* instructs its bank to send funds to the payee's bank, whereas in a debit transfer, the *payee* instructs its bank to cause funds to be transferred from the payor's account into its own (the payee's) account.

ACH debit transfers have been used in innovative ways, such as in the transfer sometimes called an "electronic check." This type of transfer begins as a conventional paper check and ends as an ACH debit to the account of a consumer. In one form of electronic check, for example, a merchant captures the information on the check presented at the point of purchase and uses that information to initiate an ACH debit to the consumer's account. (See Chapter 6 for a discussion of ACH debit entries to consumer accounts.)

Chapter 2 of this book contains a broad survey of the various payment systems, including the check system and the Fedwire, CHIPS, SWIFT, and ACH systems. Subsequent chapters discuss each of these systems in greater detail. The advent of the Internet has had an enormous impact on commerce; commerce in cyberspace and payment-related aspects of cyberspace commerce are discussed in Chapter 7. Chapter 8 concludes the book with suggestions for the management of risks, including a discussion of transactional risk and the risk of system disruptions, as well as the risks directly associated with each of the payment systems discussed in this book.

LIABILITY FOR FRAUD LOSSES: THE LAW AND THE CONTRACT WITH THE BANK

Among the risks discussed in this book, special emphasis is given to the risk of fraud. We believe that corporate management is better able to manage the risk of fraud if management has a basic understanding of how the law determines liability for fraud among the parties involved in a payment transaction.

When a fraudulent check or funds transfer is paid and the wrongdoer has escaped, which party is liable for the loss? The company whose account has been charged? The paying bank? A bank that acted as an intermediary bank? This book is not a legal treatise, but is intended to help the reader understand broadly how the law allocates liability for fraud losses to the parties in payment transactions.

The law governing checks, bank deposits, and collections is contained in Articles 3 and 4 of the Uniform Commercial Code (U.C.C). The law governing wire transfers is contained in U.C.C 4A. Automated clearing house (ACH) transfers are also governed by the ACH Rules of the National Automated Clearing House Association. These laws and rules are discussed in Chapters 3 through 6 of this book.

An understanding of the U.C.C. and ACH rules, however, is not sufficient. The treasury manager should know that these rules can be varied by the agreement of the parties. In other words, the rules generally allow the parties to agree to their own, different rules.

Bank Shifting Its Statutory Liability to the Customer: Examples

Banks typically offer their customers blanket agreements covering all of the services they provide and additional agreements that cover particular services, such as a funds-transfer agreement and an ACH Agreement. The customer should be aware that these agreements commonly impose rules that are different from the statutory rules, and that these differences are unfavorable to the customer. The differences, moreover, are typically worded indirectly and thus not clearly evident to the reader.

Consider the following examples. Note the effect as to corporate payment risk management.

Example 1, as to checks: A provision stating, "The Bank shall have no liability unless the Bank's conduct shall have constituted gross negligence or willful misconduct," may sound innocuous and reasonable, but it would *impose liability for a fraudulent check on the customer even though the customer's conduct has been blameless and the law would otherwise have imposed liability on the bank.*

Example 2, as to funds transfers: A requirement in the bank's "standard" form of funds-transfer agreement, that the customer report fraudulent or erroneous transfers within a specified period, may seem appropriate as a means of causing the customer to reconcile its bank statements promptly, as it should. The result of the requirement, however, may be *to impose liability on the customer for fraud or errors even when the bank has been at fault and the customer's conduct has been blameless.*

The bank's corporate customer may decide knowingly to agree to assume liability that the law would otherwise impose on the bank. We believe that the corporate customer, however, should be wary of assuming that liability *unwittingly*, that is, because it is ignorant of the rules or ignorant of provisions in the bank's agreement that vary the rules. That belief is reiterated in Chapters 3 through 6.

NEW FRONTIER IN CYBERSPACE

Payment by electronic means is considerably less expensive than payment by check and probably more secure. We have supported and looked forward to a general migration of business payments from the check system to paperless payment methods. The advent of the Internet and the opening of the new frontier in the payment world in cyberspace seemed to make this prospect an exciting one.

The anticipated migration to paperless payments has not yet occurred, however. Although electronic payments have increased substantially as a percentage of the dollar volume of all payments, the number of checks has not significantly dwindled. Thus, corporate and treasury managers and financial professionals still need to understand the risks of the check system as well as the risks of the paperless payment systems. It is hoped that this book will contribute to the reader's understanding of these systems.

2

Payment Systems Survey

This chapter provides a concise history of various payment systems—barter, coins, drafts, and notes—and how drafts and notes became paper money and evolved to fiat money. Checks, wire transfers, automated clearing houses, and global funds-transfer systems, the principal payment systems in use today, are covered in separate chapters in this book. Chapter 8 discusses the management of corporate payment systems risk.

BARTER

Ancient commerce used barter, the exchange of one kind of goods for another—for example, one bushel of wheat for a cow. In many locales, barter was replaced by a specific measure of a commodity as the medium of exchange. For instance, the ancient Israelites paid for goods with cattle.

COINS

Historically, the use of specific measures of precious metals replaced most bartering of commodities, with ingots and then coins coming into use. The issuance of Assyrian silver pieces at about 700 B.C. is an early example of a government issuing an official currency. The Greek city-states, and then the Persian, Alexandrian, and Roman Empires, developed and improved the system of precious-metal-based official currency. By the late Middle Ages, the payment system in Europe was based on precious metal coins, minted by powerful rulers or municipalities.

PAPER MONEY

The use of bills and notes avoids the problem of debasement. Bills of exchange—now called drafts—and promissory notes issued by depositories of precious metals in England evolved into paper money.

Drafts Become Paper Money

Metal coins are portable but heavy. In late medieval and Renaissance Europe, the short supply and bulky weight of coins impeded the growing transnational trade among merchants and could not provide the larger transactional amounts required.

The merchants invented the *bill of exchange*, today called a *draft*. As a medium of payment, these paper bills of exchange were easily portable and a highly satisfactory solution to the problem of robbery. Bills of exchange supplemented the metallic currencies of Europe during this period. Today, **paper drafts** (mostly in the form of checks) and paper money are still supplemented by coinage.

A *draft* is an instruction from one person, the draft's *drawer*, to another person, its *drawee*, to make a payment—paying either to the drawer or to a third person, the *payee* of the draft. A check, the most common form of draft in use today, is a draft drawn on a bank (see Exhibit 2.1). If a draft is negotiable, a holder of the

8

Exhibit 2.1   MICR Check

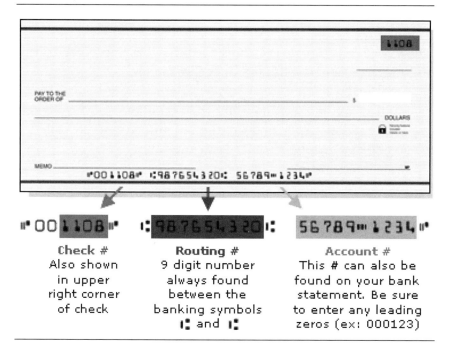

Check #	Routing #	Account #
Also shown in upper right corner of check	9 digit number always found between the banking symbols ⑂ and ⑂	This # can also be found on your bank statement. Be sure to enter any leading zeros (ex: 000123)

draft may transfer it and the transferee may present it to the drawee for payment. The negotiable draft can function much like money.

The drawer's signature on the draft says that the drawer's credit supports payment of the draft. If the drawee has undertaken to pay or "accepts" paying the draft at a later date, the drawee must pay the draft on the due date. If the drawee fails to pay, however, the payee may have recourse to the drawer—or recourse may have been waived or disclaimed. The mercantile community is thus able to value drafts according to the credit rating of the drawer—or, if payment is instead undertaken or accepted by the drawee, the drawee's credit rating substitutes for that of the drawer.

The draft is thus a flexible instrument and made much more so by its negotiability. If the original payee transfers a negotiable draft, the transferee will succeed to the rights of the transferor.

The transferee may transfer the draft to a subsequent transferee or may present the draft to the drawee. If the drawee has accepted the draft, the drawee is obliged to pay the transferee. If the drawee fails to pay, the transferee may have recourse to the original payee and the drawer, or recourse may have been waived or disclaimed.

A bill of exchange containing the acceptance of the drawee to pay the bill at a specified time in the future is today called a *time draft* or an *acceptance draft*.[1] For example, a *banker's acceptance* is a draft that substitutes the accepting bank's drawee credit rating for the rating of the drawer. Often the accepting bank is a secured lender of the drawer and is thus willing to offer its credit as accepting drawee. For the holder of the banker's acceptance, the risk is the bank's credit.

Historically, if the drawer of a bill of exchange did not have a good or known credit rating but the drawee did, the acceptance of the bill by the drawee strongly supported the negotiability of the bill. A bill of exchange accepted by the drawee in a transaction in sixteenth-century Europe was an early form of a letter of credit. In a letter of credit, the drawee, typically a bank, undertakes to pay or accept a particular bill or a series of bills drawn by a particular merchant within a specified time period. The undertaking of the drawee to pay the draft supported the draft, thus allowing the draft to evolve into a form of currency—paper money.

Notes Become Paper Money

During the seventeenth century, merchants in England became accustomed to depositing their surplus metallic currencies in the Tower of London for safekeeping by the Crown. King Charles I confiscated the metal currencies to help finance the King's side of the English Civil War. The merchants reacted to the confiscation by depositing their surplus currency with London goldsmiths. Later, as a means of paying their creditors, the merchants would draw drafts, instructing the goldsmith (drawee) to pay the creditor. The merchant's draft was an early form of check.[2]

When a large amount was deposited with a goldsmith, the goldsmith might issue to the merchant a number of receipts in smaller amounts, each representing a part of the deposit and all of them together representing the entire large deposit. These receipts were promissory notes from the goldsmith to pay the merchant, and the merchant could use the notes to pay its creditors for goods or services. Thus, the notes issued by the goldsmiths constituted a form of paper money.

In 1694, Parliament created the Bank of England, and the Bank began to issue its notes to its depositors. The risk of the bank's insolvency was thought to be less than that of the goldsmiths. The English bank notes, of course, constituted paper money as we know it today.

EVOLUTION OF FIAT MONEY IN THE UNITED STATES

New York Clearing House Association

The New York Clearing House Association was the United States' first bank clearing house and has been the key to the development and stabilization of bank settlement systems in the nation. Started in 1853, its purpose was to organize and simplify the chaotic exchange and settlement process among the banks of New York City. Until the Federal Reserve System was established in 1913, the Clearing House also tried to stabilize banking and currency fluctuations through the recurring national monetary panics.

In the early nineteenth century, New York City banks settled their accounts by hiring porters who traveled from bank to bank, exchanging checks for bags of gold coins, or "specie." The number of banks grew, and porter exchanges became a daily event.

In 1831, Albert Gallatin, past Secretary of the Treasury and President of the National Bank of New York, wrote that the lack of a daily exchange of drafts among banks "produces relaxations, favors improper expansions and is attended with serious inconveniences." On August 18, 1853, George D. Lyman, a bank bookkeeper, published an article proposing that banks send and

11

receive checks at a central office and asked that other bank cashiers contact him if they supported his idea. They did, the clearing house was established, and on its first day in October 1853, the clearing house exchanged checks worth $22.6 million.

The clearing house brought order to a tangled web of exchanges. Specie certificates soon replaced gold for settling clearing house balances. Porters were exposed to far fewer dangers than when they had transported bags of gold from bank to bank. Certificates eased the probability of a run on a bank's deposits. The clearing house required member banks to participate in weekly audits, maintain minimum reserve levels, and settle balances on a daily basis.

Clearing House Loan Certificates: A Form of Currency. Between 1853 and 1913, the United States experienced rapid economic expansion, as well as many financial panics. When specie payments were suspended, Clearing House Loan Certificates became a form of currency, not backed by gold but instead by county and state bank notes held by clearing house member banks. Bearing the words "Payable Through The Clearing House," a Clearing House Loan Certificate was the joint liability of all the member banks. The Clearing House Loan Certificates may have violated the federal law against privately issued currencies, but, as a contemporary observer noted, "performed so valuable a service . . . in moving the crops and keeping business machinery in motion, that the government . . . wisely forbore to prosecute."[3]

Federal Reserve and Fiat Money. In 1913, Congress enacted the Federal Reserve Act, which created an independent, federal clearing system modeled on the private clearing houses. The new federal reserve monetary system had stringent audits and minimum reserve standards and thus was designed to replace the role of private interbank clearing houses in reducing the nation's fears during financial panics.

The Federal Reserve Notes issued pursuant to the Act quickly became popular, but they were not made legal tender until 1933.

12

"Legal tender" denotes that an obligee must accept the tendered note to discharge the obligation of the obligor. Under current law, United States coins and currency (including Federal Reserve Notes and circulating notes of Federal Reserve banks and national banks) are legal tender for all debts, public charges, taxes, and dues. Foreign gold or silver coins are not legal tender for debts.[4] Every bill in the United States is labeled "Federal Reserve Note" and contains the legend:

This Note is legal tender for all debts, public and private.[5]

Gradually, the United States and the other major countries of the global economy in the latter part of the twentieth century replaced the gold standard with "fiat" paper money, that is, with paper money not backed by reserve holdings of precious metal. In 1965, the United States eliminated the requirement that gold reserves back Federal Reserve deposits, and in 1968 eliminated the requirement that gold reserves back Federal Reserve Notes. Finally, in 1971, the United States terminated the obligation to convert dollars held by foreign governments into gold. President Nixon, it was said, "closed the gold window."

The closing of the gold window eliminated the pretense of the United States' being on a gold standard and marked a historic change in the global payment system. Prior to 1971, all of the world's major currencies were tied, at least nominally, to a commodity. Commodity-based currencies have been a feature of payment systems since the transition, aeons ago, from barter economies. Since 1971, however, no major currency has been tied to a commodity.

Money today is fiat money—legal tender not redeemable in gold or any other specie by the government that has issued it. The Federal Reserve System and other central banks may still carry entries on their balance sheets for gold valued at a fixed price, but such an entry is "simply the smile of a vanished Cheshire cat."[6]

In Western Europe, a single monetary system is now in place for 11 countries, marking the first time these Europeans have shared a payment system since the fall of the Western Roman Empire approximately 1,500 years ago. On January 1, 1999, the 11 European countries tied their exchange rates to the Euro and gave to the new European Central Bank the power to establish interest rates and dictate monetary policy.

CHECK SYSTEMS

The ubiquitous check has a long history, and a lot of machinery and technology has been invented for processing checks. The paper check is the oldest and most frequently used noncash payment instrument in the United States.

The legal rules that govern the rights and obligations of drawers, drawees, and holders of checks today are essentially the same as those that applied in earlier periods to bills of exchange. Chapter 3, about check systems and the Uniform Commercial Code (U.C.C.), discusses the operation, the governing law, and the risks of check systems.

In the United States, before the automation of proof machines and clearing systems, checks were processed manually. Many banks would honor "counter checks," checks that did not have preprinted customer account data but carried only the name and address of the bank. Counter checks were available at merchants' counters in the community for the use of bank customers. Mechanical "proof" machines were used to sort the checks into bins for "drawn on us" and "drawn on other" banks and, for bin categories, listed amounts and total.

Each bank prepared remittance letters containing checks drawn on other banks that its customers had deposited. These remittance letters were mailed to the bank's "correspondent bank" in each geographic location; the letters requested payment for the checks contained therein. Upon receipt of funding from the correspondent bank, the bank credited its customers' accounts with "good" or "collected" funds and then permitted the customers to withdraw such funds. Today's check processing systems are all high-speed versions of these basic processes. The premise of the depository bank's time delay for collection of funds is still embedded in the automated interbank clearing systems of today.

As the Federal Reserve System developed so that each depository was assigned a unique identification number, each customer's account also was so identified; **magnetic ink character recognition** (MICR, pronounced "mike-er") was introduced, and the basis for high-speed electronic check processing systems was established. The new high-speed electronic reading proof machines replaced their older mechanical ancestors. Electronic check presentment, by which the MICR encoding is sent electronically to paying banks, is a major technological benefit of MICR. Yet despite years of promoting electronic payment and bill presentment systems, checks are still being used for most consumer-to-business payments.

ELECTRONIC PAYMENTS

Fedwire

The unique feature of Fedwire[7] is immediate finality of payment. This immediate settlement is, at present, different from any other payment system in the United States. The Federal Reserve System (the "Fed") guarantees (under Regulation J) payment to the receiving bank and assumes the credit risk of the sending bank's insufficiency of funds. The Fed mitigates that risk by delaying the execution of payment orders sent by banks that are thought to be among those that are less stable.

Since 1918, the Fed has moved funds through electronic communication systems. When the Fed changed from weekly to daily settlements, the Federal Reserve Banks installed a private telegraph system among themselves to process transfers of funds. In the 1920s, United States Treasury securities became transferable by telegraph. The nation's funds and securities transfer system remained largely telegraphic until the early 1970s. New computer technologies then became available. The Fedwire electronic transfer system was developed and is operated by the Federal Reserve System. Until 1980, Fedwire services were offered without explicit cost to Federal Reserve member commercial banks. The Depository Institutions Deregulation and Monetary Control Act of 1980 (also requiring the pricing of Fed services, including funds and securities transfers) gave nonmember depository institutions direct access to the transfer system.

The Fedwire system connects Federal Reserve Banks and Branches, the Treasury and other government agencies, and more than 9,000 on-line and off-line depository institutions. Fedwire and CHIPS (Clearing House Interbank Payment System) handle most large-dollar transfers involving the United States. Fedwire plays a key role in the nation's payments and government securities transfer mechanisms. Depository institutions use Fedwire to transfer funds to correspondent banks and to send wire transfers of their customers' funds to other institutions. Transfers on behalf of bank customers include funds used in the purchase or sale of government securities, deposits, and other large, time-sensitive payments. The Treasury and other federal agencies use Fedwire extensively to disburse and collect funds.

All Fedwire transfers are completed on the day they are initiated. The transfer is accomplished by a debit to the Federal Reserve account of the sending bank and a credit to the Federal Reserve account of the receiving bank and is final when the Fed notifies the receiving institution of the Fedwire credit to its account.

Fedwire Examples. *If the banks of the sender and receiver are in different Federal Reserve districts*, the sending bank debits the sender's account and asks its local Reserve Bank to send a transfer order to the Reserve Bank serving the receiver's bank. The two Reserve Banks settle with each other through the Interdistrict Settlement Fund, a bookkeeping system that records Federal Reserve interdistrict transactions. Finally, the receiving bank notifies the recipient of the transfer and credits the recipient's bank account. When the wire transfer is received, the receiver may use the funds immediately.

If the sending and receiving banks are in the same Federal Reserve district, the transaction is similar, but all of the processing and accounting are done by one Reserve Bank.

Net Settlement Services

In addition to Fedwire, the Federal Reserve Banks provide net settlement services for participants in private-sector payment systems, such as check clearing houses, automated clearing house associations, and private electronic funds-transfer systems that normally process a large number of transactions between member institutions. "Net settlement" involves posting net debit and net credit entries provided by such organizations to the accounts their depository institutions maintain at the Federal Reserve.

CHIPS

Fedwire and a private-sector funds-transfer network, the Clearing House Interbank Payment System (CHIPS), handle most large-dollar wire transfers. Most CHIPS transfers result from international transactions. CHIPS processes international payments electronically and is the primary system for transferring U.S. dollars between the world banks, into and out of the United States.

The CHIPS system is estimated to process about 95% of the U.S. dollar payments that move between the United States and countries around the world. Eurodollar transfers, foreign exchange, and foreign trade transactions are effected via CHIPS's electronic transmissions. (About 182,000 interbank transfers valued at nearly $1.2 trillion are made daily through the network.[8] These transfers represent about 90% of all interbank transfers relating to international U.S. dollar payments.[9]) A special Fedwire escrow account at the Federal Reserve Bank of New York enables same-day settlement of transfers.

The New York Clearing House Association organized CHIPS in 1970, and participation expanded gradually to include other commercial banks, Edge Act Corporations, United States agencies and branches of foreign banks, Article XII investment companies, and private banks. CHIPS initially utilized a next-day settlement system and in 1991 adopted a system that settled on the same day at the end of each day, but now CHIPS employs a continuous real-time, continuously matched, multilateral netting settlement system.

Each participating bank is required to prefund its fund transfers at the opening of the CHIPS business day in an amount at least equal to the participant's "opening position," which is an amount determined by the President of CHIPS, at least once each month, in accordance with a formula devised by the Clearing House. The CHIPS computers track all increases and decreases in the opening position of the participant, and thereafter throughout the day to reflect the participant's "current position" at any given moment. No payment instruction is released if its release would cause either the sending participant's or the receiving participant's position to be less than zero or to be twice the amount of its opening position.

CHIPS Funds Transfer: Example

A London importer needs to pay US$ 1,000,000 to a U.S. exporter. The importer instructs its London bank to charge its account for the Pounds Sterling equivalent of US$ 1,000,000 and to pay the exporter at New York bank "B." The London bank needs to transfer $1 million from its account at one New York correspondent bank "A" to an account at a second New York correspondent bank "B." Banks "A" and "B" are both CHIPS participants. The London bank sends bank "A" a payment instruction by telex or through the SWIFT system. (See the discussion of SWIFT later in this chapter.) Bank "A" verifies the London bank's message, then prepares and releases the data to CHIPS. The CHIPS computer verifies that the transaction is permissible and transmits the message to "B." If any credit limit is exceeded, the message is rejected. The CHIPS computer creates a record of the transaction and the debits and credits for the CHIPS records. When bank "B" receives a CHIPS credit message for one of its respondents, bank "B" notifies that bank that the funds are being credited to its account.

ACH

In the early 1970s, the rapid growth in check processing volumes and capabilities of the large new computer systems gave rise to the concept of an automated clearing house (ACH). By 1974, a national association was formed—the National Automated Clearing House Association (NACHA). Through their regional facilities, the Federal Reserve Banks provide facilities, equipment, and staff for the regional ACH networks. The local ACHs are electronically linked.

ACH operating entities (ACH Operators) are normally Federal Reserve Banks but may be private companies such as the American Clearing House Association, Electronic Payment Network, an affiliate of the New York Automated Clearing House, and VisaNet ACH Services. ACH Operators receive, edit, and process electronic entries received either from other ACH Operators or from **Originating Depository Financial Institutions (ODFIs)** and then provide settlement between the ODFIs and the **Receiving Depository Financial Institutions (RDFIs)**. ACH Operators provide a nationwide ACH system accessible to all depository financial institutions. As fiscal agents of the United States, the Federal Reserve Banks provide electronic payment services for the Treasury's ACH-based program for direct deposit of federal recurring payments such as Social Security, Veterans Administration benefits, and federal salary payments.

As part of the Monetary Control Act of 1980, private-sector ACH Operators were encouraged to compete with the Federal Reserve Banks. The Act provided that Federal Reserve Banks could no longer offer competing services free of charge and were required to charge enough to recover operating costs. A "private sector adjustment factor" is included in the processing fees in an effort to level the playing field to a "for profit" basis. Transactions between private sector ACH Operators and Federal Reserve Bank ACH Operators are governed by the interregional deposit and presentment times outlined in Federal Reserve operating circulars. Private sector ACH Operators exchange transactions among themselves according to deposit and distribution schedules to which they agree.

The parent organization, NACHA, provides oversight and guidance to America's largest electronic payments network. Most important, NACHA writes, revises, and maintains the ACH Operating Rules and Guidelines. It also develops programs to increase ACH volumes and has educational services for its members and the users of the ACH system. Regional ACHs are responsible for local rules and also provide education and services to help link all types of financial institutions—commercial banks, savings banks, and credit unions.

SWIFT

Why SWIFT Is "Swift"

SWIFT (Society for Worldwide International Financial Telecommunications) is a nonprofit society organized under Belgian law. SWIFT, which began operations in the late 1970s, is owned and used by its member banks throughout the world. The SWIFT standards and communication system enable the secure exchange of messages about financial transactions, thus facilitating swift and secure transfers of international funds.

How the SWIFT System Works

A sending bank sends instructions for payment to a SWIFT access point in the sender's country. The message is then relayed from the access point to a processor, from the processor to a SWIFT access point in the country of the receiving bank, and from that access point to the receiving bank. The receiving bank acknowledges the message and pays the beneficiary.

SWIFT is a communication system only and does not play any part in the settlement between sending and receiving banks. Settlement is typically achieved by debits and credits to "due from" or "nostro" accounts, and "due to" or "vostro" accounts, maintained by the sending and receiving banks if the banks have a **correspondent** relationship. If the banks do not have a correspondent relationship, intermediary banks that maintain "due from" and "due to" accounts for the sending and receiving banks may be used for settlement.

Because settlement in a SWIFT funds transfer occurs outside the SWIFT system, some may question whether SWIFT should be called a funds-transfer system. The question is purely one of semantics, and the answer depends on how *funds-transfer system* is defined. SWIFT is clearly a "funds-transfer system" for purposes of U.C.C. Article 4A, which includes in the definition of a funds-transfer system any "association of banks through which a payment order by a bank may be transmitted to the bank to which the order is addressed."[10]

The SWIFT system is fast, inexpensive, and available to users every day, 24 hours a day. Transmissions are typically concluded in minutes—"swiftly."

ENDNOTES

1. "Acceptance means the drawee's signed agreement to pay a draft as presented. It must be written on the draft and may consist of the drawee's signature alone." U.C.C. § 3-409(a).
2. See Benjamin Geva, *The Law of Electronic Funds Transfers*, (Matthew Bender, 1992), § 1.02[3].
3. New York Clearing House, Historical Perspective; www.nych.org/files/nych_hist.pdf, p. 2.
4. 31 U.S.C. § 5103. See regulations at 31 C.F.R. § 100.2.

5. The Federal Reserve note is authorized in § 16 of the Federal Reserve Act (12 U.S.C. §§ 411 *et seq.*).
6. Milton Friedman, *Money Mischief: Episodes in Monetary History* (San Diego, CA: Harcourt Trade Publishers, 1994).
7. Information from FedPoint43, Internet, Federal Reserve Bank of New York, July 1999.
8. Information from FedPoint36, Internet, Federal Reserve Bank of New York, July 1999.
9. *Id.*
10. U.C.C. § 4A-105(a)(5).

3

Checks and the Risk of Fraud

This chapter discusses the law of negotiable instruments, the application of the legal doctrine of a "holder in due course" to checks, the check system in the United States, how the risk of fraud is allocated to the parties participating in a check transaction, and how to manage that risk.

NEGOTIABLE INSTRUMENTS

A negotiable instrument is either a *promise* to pay a fixed sum of money or an *order* to pay a fixed sum of money. If the negotiable instrument is a promise to pay, it is a *note,* which is beyond the scope of this book. If the negotiable instrument is an order to pay, it is a *draft,* and if the draft is drawn on a bank, it is typically also a *check.*

The primary risk associated with checks is the risk of fraud. A principal goal of the law governing a negotiable instrument is to make the negotiable instrument freely transferable in commercial transactions. To further that goal, the law generally allows a person who has taken the negotiable instrument "in due course"—the "holder in due course"—to demand payment from the drawer even if fraud may have been committed by the original payee in the underlying transaction.

This chapter considers protection from fraud, under the Uniform Commercial Code (U.C.C.), to the holder in due course of a check. It also considers how the U.C.C. allocates liability for check fraud and check theft among the various parties: the bank customer who issued the check, subsequent holders of the check, and the drawee bank that is instructed to pay the check.

Drafts

A draft is a three-party instrument. The parties are the drawer, the drawee, and the payee. When the drawee is a bank, the draft is also a check. In a draft, the drawer instructs the drawee to pay the payee. What makes the draft unique is that the payee does not have to present the draft to the drawee. Instead, the payee may transfer the draft to another party, who may either present the draft for payment to the drawee or transfer the draft to yet another party. If the transferor observes the appropriate formalities, such a transfer is called "negotiation." Because a draft can be negotiated any number of times, it can support an unlimited number of transactions. An example of a draft is shown in Exhibit 3.1.

In Exhibit 3.1, the drawer is ABC Inc. The payee is XYZ Corp. The Drawee in the example is simply named "Drawee." A draft drawn on a bank is also a check unless it is a documentary draft.

A "documentary" draft is one that is presented with the expectation that specified documents, securities, or the like are to be received by the drawee as a condition to payment. In a typical letter of credit, the drawer, the beneficiary of the credit, names itself as the payee and presents the draft and other documents specified in the credit to the drawee, the bank that has issued the credit. The bank is permitted, under the credit, to pay the beneficiary's draft only if the documents presented to the

Exhibit 3.1   Draft Example

```
[Draft Date]
        To: Drawee
Pay to XYZ Corp. or order
$xxxx.yy


ABC Inc.
By: Illegible Signature
```

bank are those that have been specified in the letter of credit. In this chapter, it should be assumed that the draft is not a documentary credit except as otherwise indicated.

In Exhibit 3.1, note the wording "Pay to XYZ Corp. *or order.*" Because the draft is a negotiable instrument payable to the order of XYZ Corp., XYZ Corp. can negotiate the draft by endorsement and transfer of possession. The payee endorses the draft by signing it.

An endorsement to a named person is a *special endorsement.* An endorsement that does not name the transferee is a *blank endorsement.* In the case of a blank endorsement, any person in possession of the draft may enforce the draft by negotiating it or presenting it for payment to the drawee. If the draft is specially endorsed to a named payee, only that named payee may enforce the instrument.

When a draft is negotiated, the transferor negotiates the draft to the transferee by endorsement and delivery of possession to the transferee. In the preceding example, XYZ Corp. may negotiate the draft by special endorsement to Payee 1, Payee 1 may negotiate it by special endorsement to Payee 2, Payee 2 may negotiate it by special endorsement to Payee 3, and Payee 3 may present the draft to the drawee for payment. The endorsements on the back of the check may then appear as shown in Exhibit 3.2.

Exhibit 3.2 Endorsement Example

Payee 1 endorses "to order of" Payee 2

Payee 2 endorses "to order of" Payee 3

Payee 3 endorses by signature and
presents the draft to Drawee for payment

Answering a few simple questions can help in understanding the fundamental rules of drafts:

- *Does a merchant have to accept a draft in lieu of payment in currency?* Of course not. Assume that ABC Inc. has issued the draft, in the form of a check drawn on Rock Rib Bank of Vermont, to XYZ Corp. to satisfy an obligation to pay for merchandise purchased by ABC Inc. from XYZ Corp. XYZ Corp. has every right to refuse to accept the check and demand payment in dollars.

    If, however, XYZ Corp. accepts the check from ABC Inc., the obligation of ABC Inc. to pay XYZ Corp. for the merchandise is "suspended." If XYZ Corp. presents the draft for payment to the Rock Rib Bank and the drawee declines to pay it because of insufficient funds or for any other reason, the obligation of ABC Inc. to pay XYZ Corp. for the merchandise is revived. The drawer is liable to the payee when the drawee declines to pay the instrument.

    Suppose that instead of presenting the check for payment, ABC Inc. negotiates it to Payee 2, Payee 2 negotiates it to Payee 3, and the check is presented for payment by Payee 3 as shown in the preceding instance. If the Rock Rib Bank declines to pay Payee 3, Payee 3 may look for payment to ABC Inc., the drawer, and to all prior endorsers—that is, to Payee 1 and Payee 2—Payee 2 can look for payment to ABC Inc. and Payee 1, and Payee 1 (XYZ Corp.) to ABC Inc.

The holder of the check has *recourse* to the person who negotiated the check to the holder, to all prior endorsers, and to the drawer. An endorser has recourse to prior endorsers and the drawer. However, the holder and endorsers do not have recourse to an endorser that endorsed the check without recourse, that is, by adding the words "without recourse" to its endorsement.

- *Is the drawee obligated to the original payee or a subsequent holder to pay the draft?* Certainly not, as a general rule. In our example, the Rock Rib Bank has no contractual relationship with XYZ Corp. and may decline to pay for any reason. However, the bank has a contractual relationship with its customer, ABC Inc. If the bank wrongfully declines to pay the check and there are sufficient funds in ABC Inc.'s account to cover the check, the bank can be liable to ABC Inc. for any damages that ABC Inc. may sustain by reason of the nonpayment.

  A drawee may also agree to pay the draft at a later time—a *time draft*. The drawee manifests that agreement by signing, or "accepting," the draft. If the drawee is a merchant and the draft is issued to evidence the merchant's obligation to pay for goods, the accepted draft is a *trade acceptance*. If the drawee is a bank, the draft is a *banker's acceptance*. Absent the agreement of the drawee to pay a "sight draft" (payable at sight) or accept a "time draft" (payable at a stated later date) as in the case of a letter of credit, the drawee has no obligation to the payee or a subsequent holder of a draft to pay it.

- *If the drawee declines to pay a draft drawn on it, what are the rights of the holder of the draft? What about stop payment?* In the example, ABC Inc. is the drawer of a check drawn on the Rock Rib Bank. The check embodies a trade debt of ABC Inc. to XYZ Corp. If XYZ Corp. presents the check to the bank for payment and the bank declines to pay XYZ Corp.,

XYZ Corp. is still entitled to payment from ABC Inc., for two reasons. First, XYZ Corp. is entitled to payment of the trade indebtedness in the underlying transaction for the sale of merchandise. Second, XYZ Corp. is entitled to payment on the draft. As noted earlier, the payee of a draft is entitled to payment from the drawer when the drawee declines to pay it.

Assume, however, that the merchandise that XYZ Corp. delivered to ABC Inc. was not the merchandise that ABC Inc. had ordered. ABC Inc. can assert XYZ Corp.'s breach of its obligation under the sales contract as a defense to its obligation as drawer to pay XYZ Corp. as the payee of the draft. If the check has not yet been presented to the bank, ABC Inc. can contact the bank and ask the drawee not to pay the draft upon presentment—in other words, the drawer can ask the drawee to stop payment on the check.

- *What if the draft has been negotiated?* Suppose that XYZ Corp. has agreed to sell merchandise to ABC Inc. for $100,000. To pay for the merchandise, ABC Inc. has sent its check, drawn on Rock Rib Bank and payable to XYZ Corp. for $100,000. In an unrelated transaction, XYZ Corp. is indebted to Ajax Suppliers, Inc. for $300,000. In partial payment of that indebtedness, XYZ Corp. endorses the ABC Inc. check by writing "Pay to the order of Ajax Suppliers, Inc." and sends the check to Ajax. Subsequently, the merchandise arrives at ABC Inc., and ABC Inc. discovers that the merchandise is defective. ABC Inc. has a "defense to payment" (legalese for a "reason not to pay") against XYZ Corp., and it calls the Rock Rib Bank and stops payment on the check.

Ajax then presents the check to ABC Inc. Can ABC Inc., as the drawer of the check, assert its defense to payment against the original payee against Ajax, a subsequent holder of the check? Ajax took the check in good faith and without knowledge of ABC Inc.'s defense to payment against XYZ Corp. Must ABC Inc. pay Ajax?

The answer is yes. When Ajax took the draft in good faith in order to discharge, in part, the debt owed to it by XYZ Corp., it became a "holder in due course." It is a fundamental principle of draft law that a holder in due course is immune to (not "infected by") any defense to payment that the drawer of the draft may have against the original payee of the draft.

Check Law

A check is a draft drawn on a bank. Thus, all of the preceding discussion in regard to the law of drafts applies to checks. All checks are drafts, except that a documentary draft (described earlier) is not a check even when the drawee is a bank.

Drafts and checks are subject to the law of drafts under Article 3 of the U.C.C. and subject to the law of bank deposits and collections under U.C.C. Article 4. The Articles of the U.C.C. are model laws drafted by a national council that sponsors the U.C.C. and presents the models to the state legislatures for adoption, with the goal that the commercial laws in the 50 states be "uniform" and not vary from state to state.

SOME DEFINITIONS

The *drawer* of the check is the customer of the bank. The drawer writes the check. The *drawee* is always the bank. The *payee* of the check is entitled to present the check for payment to the bank and to do so is required to mail or deliver it, or cause it to be delivered, to the drawee bank. Typically, the payee deposits the check at its own bank, which then causes the check to be presented to the drawee bank.

The first bank in the chain of collecting a check is called the *depository bank*. The depository bank may present the check for payment to the drawee bank or send it for collection to another bank, perhaps a Federal Reserve Bank. Depository banks and other banks in the chain of collection, other than the drawee bank, are called *collecting banks*. The drawee bank is called the *payor bank*.

The delivery of a check to a collecting bank for collection—or to any other transferee with the intention that the transferee may receive funds from the payor bank—is a *transfer of the check*. The delivery of a check to the payor bank for payment is a **presentment**.

Paid and Accepted (Certified) Checks

As noted earlier, a creditor need not accept a debtor's check. The creditor may instead demand that the drawer pay in cash, deliver a cashier's check, deliver a "certified check," or use some other form of payment. If the creditor accepts the check, however, the debtor's obligation is "suspended" (deferred), and if the check is paid by the payor bank, the obligation is "discharged" (terminated). The obligation is also discharged if the bank "accepts" the check by "certifying" it—the bank stamps, dates, and signs the check as "certified" and thus guarantees to pay it. (When a bank certifies a check, it usually reserves the funds from the drawer's bank account.)

What If a Check "Bounces"? If the bank "dishonors" a check—refuses to pay it—the "suspension" of the obligation of the drawer to the payee stops and the holder of the check may then again demand payment from the drawer. If the drawer declines to pay the check, the holder may bring an action against the drawer "on the instrument." In an action on the instrument, the holder asserts the drawer's obligation to pay as the drawer of a dishonored check.

The drawer—the person who wrote the check—may be able to avoid liability on the check if the holder demanding payment is the original payee; for example, if the holder is the seller and the goods or services delivered were not as represented. The drawer may not avoid liability, however, if the holder demanding payment is not the original payee but a "holder in due course."

Any person who endorsed the check is liable to any person to whom the check was subsequently endorsed unless—and this is important—the endorsement was stated to be "without recourse."

So many checks are routinely endorsed and deposited and paid on presentment that the risks of endorser liability are often not remembered or not clearly understood. *Anyone who is asked to endorse or provide a company endorsement on a check is advised to consider using an endorsement "without recourse."*

Bearer Paper

As noted earlier in respect to drafts, in a blank endorsement, the transferor endorses the check simply by signing the name of the transferor and does not identify the transferee by name. When the transferor delivers possession of the check to the transferee, the check becomes "bearer" paper, and any person in possession of the check is entitled to enforce it by negotiating it to another transferee or presenting it for payment to the drawee. To avoid the risks associated with bearer paper, the payee may use a restrictive or a special endorsement.

A *restrictive endorsement* limits payment to a particular person or prohibits further transfer or negotiation of the check. The endorsement "Pay to Josephine Jones" (instead of "*to the order of* Josephine Jones") or "For Deposit Only to Account #12345678" is a restrictive endorsement.

A *special endorsement* cannot eliminate the risk that the check will become bearer paper by reason of a subsequent transfer. Suppose, for example, that XYZ Corp. endorses the check "Pay to the order of Ajax." The endorsement is a special endorsement because only Ajax is entitled to enforce the check by negotiating it or presenting it for payment. Nothing prevents Ajax, however, from endorsing the check "in blank" by signing it without naming a transferee. For instance, if Ajax endorses the check "Ajax by Herry Glutz, President," without identifying the transferee, the check becomes bearer paper and can be enforced by any person who possesses it.

31

Negotiation and Endorsement

Negotiation is the process by which a negotiable instrument is transferred from a holder of the instrument to another holder. The "negotiation" enables a holder of the check to transfer possession of the check and make the recipient a holder. If the check is payable to the "bearer," the transfer of possession is all that is necessary for negotiation. If the check is payable to an identified entity, that entity's endorsement is needed to negotiate the check. *Endorsement* occurs when the holder signs on the reverse side of the check, typically across the top of the left side.

"Holder in Due Course" Doctrine

The holder in due course doctrine developed in England and continental Europe in post-Renaissance times to support the use of drafts by protecting a transferee of a draft from claims that the drawer may have had against the original payee. The doctrine applies to a "holder" of a "negotiable instrument." Accordingly, we consider at the outset of this discussion what is meant by a *negotiable instrument*, what is meant by a *holder*, and then what is meant by *due course.*

Negotiable Instruments. The U.C.C. distinguishes between two kinds of negotiable instruments. One kind of negotiable instrument is a note, a promise to pay. The other kind is a draft, an order by the drawer to the drawee to pay the payee. This chapter is concerned only with the latter kind of negotiable instrument. A check is a negotiable instrument because it is a draft drawn on a bank.

A negotiable instrument must contain an unconditional promise or order to pay a fixed amount of money, be payable on demand or at a definite time, and contain no other instructions from the person promising or ordering payment. A typical check satisfies these conditions. A check is a negotiable instrument regardless of whether it contains the traditional "to the order of" wording that is otherwise required of negotiable instruments.

Some Definitions

A check can be "disqualified" as a negotiable instrument if the drawer tries to instruct the drawee bank to do something other than to pay money or tries to make the check conditional. A check that is subject to another writing, for example, is conditional. Words such as "Payment is subject to the October 15, 1999, Loan Agreement" would destroy the negotiability of the check. If the drawer, however, seeks to disqualify the check as a negotiable instrument by writing "This check is not a negotiable instrument under U.C.C. Article 3," a court will ignore the writing and treat the check as a negotiable instrument if it otherwise satisfies the requirements for negotiability.

Holder. As noted earlier, if a check is payable to an identified person, the payee may negotiate the check by endorsing it and delivering possession of the check to the recipient, who thereby becomes a holder. Collecting banks typically become holders of checks in this manner. Thus, if XYZ Corp., as the payee of a check, endorses the check and delivers possession of the check to Ajax Corporation, Ajax becomes the holder of the check.

Under the 1990 revisions to U.C.C. Article 3, the requirement that the check be endorsed in order for the transferee to become a holder does not apply to the deposit of a check by a holder into the depository bank. When the holder of the check deposits the check into the depository bank for collection, the bank becomes a holder regardless of whether the check was endorsed. Thus, endorsement of checks "For deposit only to . . ." is not required of depository banks for lockbox processing. In the example, Ajax Corporation may deposit the check into its bank account without endorsing it.

Risk Mitigation for a Holder. If a holder of a check cannot timely deposit the check, placing a restrictive endorsement (such as "For deposit only") will prevent a third party from claiming to be a holder—by forged endorsement or otherwise. It is important to note that a holder is entitled to enforce the check. This means that the holder may transfer the check to a subsequent holder

33

(who may be a collecting bank) or present the check for payment at a counter of the payor bank. If the check is dishonored, the holder may enforce the check by presenting it for payment to any previous endorser—other than an endorser that signed and added the words "without recourse"—or to the drawer.

Due Course

Apparent Authenticity. A holder does not hold a check "in due course" if the check bears apparent evidence of forgery or alteration or otherwise appears so "irregular" or incomplete so as to call into question its authenticity. In other words, the check must appear to be authentic. If it does not appear to be authentic when the recipient receives the check, the holder is not a holder in due course.

A check may be so incomplete or so irregular as to alert the recipient that it may not be authentic. The mere fact that a check is incomplete, however, is not necessarily an indication that it is not authentic. Suppose, for example, that a buyer and a seller of goods wish to consummate a transaction a week after the delivery of the buyer's check, but they are not certain of the quantity of the goods that will be available on the transaction date. The buyer delivers a signed check to the seller leaving the amount blank. The U.C.C. allows the seller to fill in the amount of the check.

If the seller completes the amount by filling in an amount that is not authorized, the check is treated as one that has been fraudulently altered. If, for example, the seller fills in an amount that is 10 times the appropriate price for the quantity of goods delivered, the buyer may assert a claim for fraud against the seller—but *(big risk here)* the buyer has no claim against the depository bank, other collecting banks, the payor bank, or any other person who has given value for the check. A bank or other holder that takes the check would be a holder in due course. The rule would apply even if the incomplete check were stolen from the buyer and completed by the thief. This explains the old rule: Never give anyone a "blank check"!

An irregular check is one that would reasonably be expected to make the person taking it suspicious. For example, if a check is illegible, is unusually backdated, or bears a signature that is an "X," a bank accepting the check for deposit or other person taking the check may not be a holder in due course, nor would a transferee be a holder in due course through endorsement.

For Value.   To be a holder in due course, the holder must have taken the instrument for value; that is, the holder must have paid for the check or otherwise sustained or committed to sustain an out-of-pocket loss or liability.

Good Faith.   A holder in due course must have taken the instrument in "good faith." The essence of good faith is honesty. A holder acts in good faith when its conduct constitutes "honesty in fact." In addition, under the 1990 revisions to Article 3, the good faith requirement obliges the holder to comply with "reasonable commercial standards of fair dealing." Thus, the holder's conduct cannot be construed to have been in good faith if a reasonable holder would have behaved in a different manner, even though the holder whose conduct is tested may have believed that the conduct was honest.

NOTICE OF FRAUD OR DEFENSES TO PAYMENT

A holder may not qualify as a holder in due course when it has notice of certain problems associated with a check. The notice that disqualifies the holder includes knowledge that:

- The drawee bank has already dishonored the check,
- The check contains an unauthorized signature or has been altered,
- Another person has a claim to the check, or
- The drawer or the drawee bank has a defense to payment of the check.

For example, suppose a buyer delivers a check to a seller as payment for goods purchased by the buyer. The buyer takes delivery from the seller, but instead of the bargained-for goods, the delivered cartons contain only worthless rocks and sand. The buyer stops payment on the check, and the seller deposits the check into its bank for collection. The depository bank grants the seller a provisional credit and presents the check to the payor bank. The payor bank dishonors the check, and the depository bank seeks to reverse the provisional credit but cannot recover the funds because the seller has become insolvent.

Under these circumstances, the depository bank would normally be a holder in due course and thus be entitled to payment from the buyer, as the drawer of the check, despite the buyer's defense of fraud against the seller. However, if the bank has notice that the buyer has a defense to payment of the check based on the seller's fraud, the bank would not be a holder in due course and thus not be entitled to enforce the check against the drawer-buyer.

Risks to Others Because of the Rights of a Holder in Due Course

The rights of a holder in due course present real risks to those who write checks, the drawers, and endorsers who do not restrict their endorsements.

The principal benefit of being a holder in due course is that the drawer of the check has virtually no defense to a demand for payment by the holder. Put another way, if the drawee fails to pay, the holder in due course is entitled to demand payment from the drawer, and the drawer must almost always pay the holder in due course.

The drawer of the check may try to avoid drawer liability—for example, by asserting that the goods that the drawer has purchased have not been delivered. So long as the holder is not aware of the relevant facts and otherwise qualifies as a holder in due course, however, the holder in due course is entitled to payment "on the instrument"; that is, the holder is entitled to be paid by the drawer of the check. The drawer may not assert the defenses to payment of the check against the holder in due course that the drawer would have under contract law against the original payee.

Suppose, for example, that a buyer draws a check to pay for what it subsequently discovers are fraudulent goods. The payee of the check—the seller who delivered the fraudulent goods—does not deposit the check at its bank. Instead, the payee endorses the check to a new holder who in good faith pays (possibly at a discount) the payee for the check. The new holder in due course can collect the amount of the check from the unhappy drawer.

The drawer of a check does have a few of what are called "real" defenses against a holder in due course. Incapacity is a real defense. The holder in due course cannot enforce payment of a check drawn by a six-year-old or a drawer who is mentally incompetent. If the drawer was induced to sign the check by fraud or under duress, the drawer can assert these facts as a real defense. If the drawer, in bankruptcy proceedings, has been discharged of its obligation to pay the check, the discharge is a real defense.

A second benefit afforded to a holder in due course is immunity from ownership claims or other claims to possession of the check. The check may have been stolen. If the check was a bearer check or the payee of the check endorsed the check prior to the theft—without a restrictive endorsement—a holder in due course of the stolen check may enforce payment of the check against the drawer, despite the theft.

As a third benefit, the holder of a check that is a negotiable instrument under U.C.C. Article 3 is afforded certain advantages in litigation. In court, the authenticity of a signature on the check is deemed to be admitted unless denied in pleadings filed with the court. If the authenticity of the signatures is either admitted or proved, the holder is entitled to judgment by the court unless the drawer has a valid defense to payment. If the holder is a holder in due course, however, even the defense to payment may not be available to the drawer.

Shelter Principle

A negotiable instrument is "transferred" when the payee or a subsequent holder delivers it to the transferee for the purpose of giving the recipient the right to enforce it—that is, the right to present it for payment or to negotiate it to a third party. An instrument that is payable to an idcntificd pcrson may bc transfcrrcd without the endorsement of the transferor. In that case, the instrument will not have been negotiated and the transferee technically will not be a "holder," much less a holder in due course. Under the rule known as the "shelter principle," however, the transfer vests in the transferee all of the rights of the transferor to enforce the check.

Thus, if the transferor is a holder in due course, the shelter principle allows the transferee to enforce the check as though it were a holder in due course even though the transferee is not a holder because the check has not been endorsed or is a holder but not in due course because, for example, the transferee paid no consideration or had knowledge of a claim or defense of the drawer. Under the shelter principle, the transferee can "take shelter" in the title of the transferor. By giving shelter to a transferee who is not a holder in due course, the law ensures the free marketability of the instrument in the hands of the transferor who is a holder in due course. The principle is also known as he principle of "derivative title" because the rights of the transferee derive from the rights of the transferor.

Although the shelter principle allows the transferee from a holder in due course to enforce the check as though the transferee were also a holder in due course, it does not afford the holder of a check the U.C.C. Article 3 advantages in litigation discussed earlier. As an exception to the shelter principle, a transferee cannot acquire the rights of a holder in due course if the transferee has engaged in fraud or illegality affecting the check.

CHECK SYSTEM IN THE UNITED STATES

Bank Deposits and Collections: The Depository Bank— Provisional versus Final Payment of a Check

When the original payee or a subsequent holder of a check deposits the check with its bank for collection, the bank usually credits the depositor's account. The credit is "provisional," however, because if the check is not paid by the payor bank or for other reasons the depository bank does not receive final payment for the check, the depository bank may charge back the credit to the customer's account. The bank's charge-back rights, however, are subject to certain time limits.

The "midnight deadline." The bank may charge back the credit and obtain the refund with impunity if it returns the check or sends notice of the facts within the bank's "midnight deadline" or—if a longer time is "reasonable"—within the longer reasonable time after its learns the facts. A bank's midnight deadline is midnight on the banking day following the banking day on which it receives the check. If the bank acts after its midnight deadline or after a longer reasonable time has expired, the bank is liable to its customer for any loss resulting from its delay.

The depository bank may present the check for payment directly to the payor bank, send the check into a check clearing house system, or send the check to another collecting bank with which it has a relationship, including a Federal Reserve Bank.

Payor Bank: "Final Settlement" of Presentments

A collecting bank normally "presents" a check or causes another collecting bank or clearing house system to present the check, that is, deliver it for payment to the payor-drawee bank. As noted earlier, the payor-drawee bank has no obligation whatever to the original payee or to any subsequent holder. The payor bank's obligations are only to its customer, the drawer of the check.

If the payor bank wrongfully dishonors a presented check and thereby causes damage to its customer, the payor bank may be liable to its customer for the damages caused by its wrongful dishonor. The payor bank has no liability, however, to the presenter of the check, to any bank in the chain of collecting banks, or to the holder who deposited the check in the depository bank, provided that (and this is important) the payor-drawee bank acts timely in dishonoring the check.

If the payor bank settles for a check (other than a check presented for payment over the counter) with the bank that presented the check by midnight on the day the check is received, it may revoke the settlement prior to its "midnight deadline"—this deadline is the same midnight deadline as the depository bank's—if it did not make "final" payment for the check by midnight of the banking day after the banking day on which the check is received.

Suppose, for example, that the depository bank sends a check to the payor bank with instructions to settle for the check by remitting a teller's check drawn on a third bank located in the city in which the depository bank is located. The payor bank sends the teller's check prior to midnight on the day on which the check was received from the depository bank. Under the rule, the payor bank is entitled to revoke the settlement and recover the payment from the depository bank if it returns the check or sends written notice of dishonor prior to its midnight deadline, that is, midnight of the day following the day the payor bank received the check.

The payor bank may not revoke its settlement, however, if it has made a "final" payment to the presenting bank. The payor bank has a statutory right under U.C.C. Article 4 to revoke a settlement by its midnight deadline.

A payor bank makes a final payment to the bank that presented the check when the payor bank pays the check in cash, settles for the check without retaining the right to revoke the settlement, or makes a provisional settlement for the check with the bank that presented it and fails to revoke the settlement within the time allowed by statute, clearing house rule, or agreement.

Technologies have facilitated the speed of check processing and made feasible the deadlines for final settlement. These technologies, as a practical matter, eliminate the "human touch" in reviewing most checks being processed. The trade-off for businesses obtaining fast final settlement in the check processing system is their assuming greater responsibility for preventing check fraud. Internal controls, timely bank reconciliation, payor notification of large-item presentments, and the use of electronic payment systems can reduce the risks of fraud and failure in the high-volume paper check system.

FRAUD AND FORGERY

Basic Rule with Respect to Fraud

The basic rule of U.C.C. Articles 3 and 4 in regard to fraud is that the payor bank is liable to its customer when the bank pays a check that has been forged or altered on its face or when the payment was not authorized but effected by fraudulent means. A forged signature is not an authorized signature, and no person is liable for the amount of a check, either as the drawer or an endorser, unless that person or an agent of that person has signed it.

A check that is not authorized is not "properly payable" under the U.C.C. Pursuant to the basic rule, the bank that pays such a check must recredit the account of its customer. The basic rule applies generally to fraud and forgery on the face of the check. Different rules apply to fraudulent endorsements.

The basic rule is however, subject to numerous exceptions. The basic rule and the exceptions are discussed in the following paragraphs. The old lawyer's joke may apply to the basic rule and its exceptions: "What the large print gives you, the small print takes away."

As noted previously, the basic rule is that a check is not properly payable by the payor bank if has not been authorized by or on behalf of the drawer. Consider, for example, Exhibit 3.3.

Many kinds of fraud are possible in the check shown in Exhibit 3.3. For example, an unauthorized employee may have forged the signature on the check. "XYZ Corp." may be a fictitious name or denote the name of a bank account maintained by a wrongdoer rather than a creditor of ABC Inc. The check may have been altered. Perhaps the check was originally in the amount of $50, but the payee has altered the amount to $500 (note that the amount of the check is not written out; instead, the numeric amount is repeated) or perhaps instead the check was made payable to "XYB Company," but the payee's name was altered to "XYZ Corp."

If the signature on the check was forged or the amount of the check was altered, the basic rule applies, and the bank is required to recredit the customer's account. If "XYZ Corp." is a fictitious name or an actual company belonging to a wrongdoing

Exhibit 3.3   Check Example

ABC Inc.	
Anywhere USA	Date: October 15, 2000

Pay to the order of _XYZ Corp. $ 500.00

500.00 and $^{no}/_{100}$ xxxxxxxxxxxxxxxxxxxxxxxxxxxxxxxxxxxxxxxxxx Dollars

Illegible Signature
Memo: _____   Authorized Signatory, ABC Inc.

employee, then any endorsement of the check in the name of XYZ Corp. is fraudulent and the check is not properly payable, but the rules regarding fraudulent endorsements, discussed later, may make ABC Inc. liable for the fraud of its employee.

Exceptions to the Basic Rule

There are two exceptions to the basic rule that the payor bank is liable when it has paid a check that was not properly payable because the signature on the face of the check was unauthorized or the payee's name or the amount of the check was altered.

Duty of the Customer to Report Fraud. The first exception to the basic rule is based on the customer's duty to report fraud. The customer must be reasonably prompt in examining its bank statement to determine whether any paid check was altered or not authorized. If, based on the bank statement, the customer should reasonably have discovered an alteration or an unauthorized check that was paid by the bank, the customer is responsible to give prompt notice of that fact to the bank.

If the customer does not give prompt notice, the customer is precluded from asserting the alteration or the unauthorized check. "Precluded" in this context means that because the customer has failed to report the check when it should have been reported, the customer cannot belatedly assert the fraud. The customer must pay the price for failing to exercise reasonable promptness in examining the statement and notifying the bank when the altered or unauthorized check was discovered.

If there is more than one unauthorized or altered check attributable to the same perpetrator, the time allowed the customer in order to avoid the preclusion rule, with respect to the second and subsequent checks, is restricted to a maximum of 30 days. Under these circumstances, the customer has a reasonable period of time, but not more than 30 days, from the date that the customer receives the statement disclosing the fraudulent check.

Customer's Failure to Exercise Ordinary Care. The second exception to the basic rule, that a payor bank is liable when it pays a check that is not properly payable because it has been altered or the drawer's signature is not authorized, applies when the customer has failed to exercise ordinary care. "Ordinary care" is a concept akin to the more familiar concept of "negligence." Ordinary care, however, is defined in the U.C.C. as the "observance of reasonable commercial standards" prevailing in the area where the person whose conduct is being examined is located for the business in which the person is engaged.

For example, suppose that a payor bank pays a check drawn on ABC Inc., and the drawer's signature on behalf of ABC Inc. is forged. As noted earlier, the check would be unauthorized and not properly payable by the bank. Suppose further, however, that the forger was a bookkeeper at ABC Inc., that the bookkeeper had served prison time for check forgery, and that ABC Inc. had hired the bookkeeper without conducting a background check. Under these circumstances, the liability of the bank for having paid a check that was not properly payable would probably shift to the customer because the customer had failed to exercise ordinary care when it hired the bookkeeper.

Comparative Fault

The 1990 revisions to U.C.C. Articles 3 and 4 refined the allocation of liability by introducing the concept of "comparative fault." Suppose in the foregoing example that the forged check was made payable to "OddlyNamedPayee" for $1,000, and the customer reports the forgery. In the following month, the bank pays a check for $2,500,000 made payable to the same "OddlyNamedPayee." The customer may argue that the bank had failed to exercise ordinary care in paying the check. The fact that the bank had reported the fraud in the preceding month, coupled with the unusually large amount of the check, might arguably have prompted a careful bank to examine the check by hand and thus discover that the payee was the payee in the previous fraud. If the court agrees that the bank had failed to exercise ordinary care, then it may assess and compare the degree to which the conduct of the customer and the conduct of the bank contributed to the loss.

Certainly, under these circumstances, the exception to the basic rule would shift liability to the customer. Although the check was not properly payable by the bank, the customer's hiring the ex-convict bookkeeper without a background check constituted a failure to exercise ordinary care.

The customer would argue, however, that the bank failed to exercise ordinary care when it paid a check in a very large amount made payable to OddlyNamedPayee, the payee of a known forged check that had been reported by the customer in the preceding month. The court may decide under these circumstances that the bank and the customer ought to share liability for the loss, either 50% to each party or on some other basis.

The concept of comparative fault also applies when the customer has failed to report the payment of an unauthorized or altered check. As noted earlier, the payor bank may avoid liability for the fraudulent check when the customer has failed to report the check. The customer must use reasonable promptness in examining the bank statement and report the check promptly after discovering it. The customer is allowed a reasonable time, not to exceed 30 days, if the check is the second in a series of fraudulent checks attributable to the same perpetrator.

If the bank has failed to exercise ordinary care in paying the check, however, the court apportions the liability. The court determines the degree to which the failure of the customer to report the loss within the allotted time contributed to the loss and the degree to which the failure of the bank to exercise ordinary care contributed to the loss.

It is important to note that the 1990 revisions to Articles 3 and 4 make clear that the mere failure of the payor bank to examine a check by sight for the purpose of detecting fraud does not constitute a failure to exercise ordinary care. When liability for the payment of a check that was not properly payable shifts to the customer, either because the customer has failed to exercise ordinary care or because the customer has failed to report the fraudulent check within the allotted time, the customer cannot claim comparative fault on the part of the bank simply because the bank did not examine the check.

Payor Bank's Recourse against Collecting Banks

To whatever extent the payor bank may be liable to the customer for a check that is not properly payable, the payor bank has no recourse to the previous banks in the chain of collection. The Uniform Commercial Code retains the rule established by an English court in the eighteenth century that the drawee bank bears the risk that the drawer's signature is unauthorized.

The reason for the rule in the eighteenth century was that the bank was expected to recognize the forgery of its customer. With automated check processing and the deadlines currently in force, that reason makes no sense today. However, the nineteenth-century rule that prevents the bank from seeking recovery against collecting banks is thought appropriate today on the grounds of finality—the notion that it is better to hold the payor bank responsible for the loss than to undo all of the transactions between the payor and the collecting banks. As noted in a later section, the rule is different when a fraudulent endorsement is involved.

Variation by Agreement: Warning to Treasury Managers and Their Lawyers

Treasury managers should be warned that the rules described previously may be varied in an agreement between the payor bank and its customer.

For example, the deposit agreement may provide: "Customer agrees to be liable for any altered, forged, or unauthorized check, even though such check is not a properly payable item under Articles 3 and 4 of the Uniform Commercial Code."

This agreement would be effective to shift liability that would otherwise be borne by the bank to the customer for the payment of a check that is not a properly payable check.

Watch out for "gross negligence and willful misconduct" clauses. The foregoing agreement would be very unusual, but treasury managers and their attorneys should be warned that liability-shifting provisions in deposit agreements are typically disguised as provisions that make the bank liable for "gross negligence" or "willful misconduct." Suppose, for example, that the deposit agreement provides, "Bank shall have no liability under this Agreement for the payment of any check except to the extent that the conduct of the bank has constituted gross negligence or willful misconduct."

This provision appears to be favorable to the customer because the bank assumes liability when its behavior has been grossly negligent or has constituted willful misconduct. In reality, however, the provision shifts liability in a typical fraud case, involving a forged or unauthorized drawer's signature or an alteration, from the bank to the customer. Not untypically, the attorney for the customer may suggest deleting the word "gross," so that the bank assumes liability for any negligence, not only "gross negligence," or the customer's attorney may suggest deleting the word "willful," so that the bank assumes liability for any misconduct, not only "willful misconduct." The attorney may deem these to be clever suggestions, but in fact they would betray his or her ignorance of check law. The bank would happily comply with these suggestions, because the provisions would shift liability for fraud under the basic rule from the bank to the customer.

There is nothing inherently wrong, of course, with a customer's agreement to assume liability that would normally be allocated to the bank under the Uniform Commercial Code. Customers traditionally do so in resolutions of their boards of directors regarding the use of facsimile signatures on checks. A customer who agrees to assume liability that would normally be borne by the bank, however, should do so with a full understanding of the legal implications and not as a result of ignorance on the part of the customer's attorney as to check liability law.

Fraudulent Endorsements

Suppose that Consultant is an occasional consultant for ABC Inc. Impersonating Consultant, Imposter causes the accounts payable department of ABC Inc. to mail a check made payable to Imposter—perhaps by sending a change of address. When the check is delivered to Imposter, Imposter endorses the check and deposits the check into Imposter's bank account. Imposter's bank pays Imposter and presents the check to ABC Inc.'s bank, which pays the check and charges ABC Inc.'s account.

The check was not properly payable out of ABC Inc.'s account, but Imposter's forged endorsement in Consultant's name would result in ABC Inc.'s being liable for the loss under the forged endorsement rules of U.C.C. Article 3. When the drawer delivers a check to an imposter impersonating the payee, an endorsement by any person in the name of the payee is effective as the endorsement of the payee in favor of any person acting in good faith who pays the check or takes it for collection.

In addition to the rule applicable to imposters described here, the fraudulent endorsement rules are generally designed to shift losses resulting from check fraud from the payor bank to the bank's customer when the fraud has been perpetrated by an employee of the customer. One of these rules then focuses on the person whose "intent determines to whom the check is payable." If the check is signed manually, the person whose "intent determines to whom the check is payable" is the signer of the check. If the check is signed by automated means, such as a check-writing machine, the person whose intent is determinative is the person who supplies the name of the payee—often an employee in the accounts payable department.

The person to whom a check is payable is determined by the intent of the person who signs the check. The person who signs the check is the person whose "intent determines to whom the check is payable," regardless of whether that person is authorized. The general rule regarding fraudulent endorsements is that when the person whose intent is determinative does not intend that the payee identified on the check have an interest in the check, any endorsement is effective as the endorsement of the payee. Suppose, for example, that Jones, an accounts payable employee, routinely supplies a list of checks to be signed by Smith, a vice president authorized to sign checks for the company. The list supplied by Jones to Smith includes a check payable to Richard Roe for $500. Smith signs the check and returns it to Jones. Jones endorses the check to himself and deposits it into his account.

In this case, the basic rule does not apply, because Smith was authorized to sign the check. The drawer's signature was thus authorized and not forged. The forged endorsement rules would apply instead of the basic rule. Jones is the person whose intent is determinative to whom the check was payable. Jones never intended that Richard Roe (whether or not he is a fictitious person) have any interest in the check. When Jones provided the list to Smith, he intended to appropriate the check for himself. Thus, Jones's endorsement is effective and cause the company, not the bank, to be liable for the fraudulent check. This rule also applies even if the person or entity shown as payee of the check is a fictitious person. Under these circumstances, the general rule for fraudulent endorsements would apply. Jones's endorsement in the name of Roe is effective against any person who in good faith pays the check or takes it for value or collection.

If, in signing the check, Smith had believed Richard Roe to be an employee of the company, this example would be illustrative of the hoary "padded payroll fraud." In any case, the example illustrates the general rule that when the person whose intent is determinative does not intend that the named payee have any interest in the check, an endorsement by any person is effective in favor of a good faith recipient of the check.

The 1990 revisions to U.C.C. Article 3 added a provision that makes any fraudulent endorsement effective when the endorsement is made by any employee of the drawer who has been entrusted with responsibility for the check. In general, the new provision would apply to the same circumstances to which the old fraudulent endorsement provisions described earlier would apply. The old provisions, however, would generally apply only to hold the drawer-employer liable when the perpetrator is an employee of the drawer. The new provision applies also to hold the payee-employer liable when the perpetrator is an employee of the payee.

Assume, for example, a $500 check payable to XYZ Corp. is received by Green, a bookkeeper at XYZ Corp. who is entrusted with the duty of posting checks received by XYZ Corp. to the appropriate accounts. Green steals the check, fraudulently endorses the check in the name of XYZ Corp., and deposits the check into the bookkeeper's personal account for collection. Under the new provisions, the fraudulent endorsement is effective and the XYZ Corp. is liable for the resulting fraud loss.

Comparative Fault as to Fraudulent Endorsements. The 1990 revisions to Article 3 added the concept of comparative fault to the provisions on fraudulent endorsements. Comparative fault is discussed earlier with respect to alterations and forged and unauthorized drawer's signatures. In the context of endorsements, if the drawer or an employer is liable for a check that has been fraudulently endorscd, but thc payor or a collecting bank has failed to exercise ordinary care, the drawer or employer may recover the loss from the bank to the extent that the failure of the bank to exercise ordinary care contributed to the loss.

Conversion. Conversion is the taking of property that belongs to another. When a check has been delivered to the payee, it becomes the property of the payee. If the check is stolen from the payee and the thief deposits the check into the thief's account at the depository bank, the depository bank is liable to the payee for conversion of the check unless the depository bank becomes a holder by negotiation of the check or unless the fraudulent endorsement rules described in the preceding section apply.

MANAGING RISKS OF THE CHECK PAYMENT SYSTEM: COMPANY THAT ISSUES CHECKS

Here the risk management of checks is viewed from the perspective of the business entity that draws and issues checks. The objective is to pay the amounts owed only to those owed. Assuming funds are available, businesses try to pay timely to protect or enhance their credit rating. Clarity of the payment details supports efficient accounting and communications by the accounts payable department of the payor and the accounts receivable departments of the payee.

Internal Controls

Good internal controls protect every honest employee. The issuer should plan and document dual controls for all aspects of issuing checks from inception and continuing through the process of reconciling bank statements. Even in businesses with a small number of finance or administrative employees, dual controls can be established involving operations personnel or owner/executives.

The following discussion indicates how a plan for dual controls, suitable to the staffing of a company, can be developed and documented. Dual control can be established using review by two people or by two different departments, or both.

Approved Vendors. Controls should be established for the approval of new vendors to the company. The entry into the computer system of new names or changes of address of the vendors authorized to receive payments from the company should also be under dual control or review. This procedure reduces the risk that checks will be issued and mailed to imposter vendors.

Payment Approvals. Before checks are issued, the invoices or other written requests for payment should be approved by a process independent of the signatory to the check. If the check signatory is also in a position to approve invoices or payments, the signatory should seek another person to approve the payments to which it will be the signatory.

Check Writing. The check stock removed from storage for check writing should be logged, as discussed under check stock; voids should also be logged.

Check Signing. The signature process may be automated under dual controls. Some companies require dual signatures on all checks or on checks over a designated amount. Very large amounts may better be paid by wire transfer or "payable through drafts," which result in the drawee bank's review prior to payment.

Bank Controls

The drawer can mitigate risks of unauthorized high-dollar withdrawal transactions (whether by check, wire, or automated clearing house, ACH) through controls at its bank. For example, the company can place a maximum dollar limit for any one transaction, for any one payee, or for any day. The bank will notify the company if excess amounts attempt to post. The company should have procedures as to who authorizes the bank to pay high-dollar exceptions, and the parameters for these arrangements should not be general knowledge within the company.

Timely Review of Bank Statements. The issuer of checks should timely review and reconcile its bank statements. The first control is to ensure that the statements are received regularly by the person responsible for the reconciliation. The person who reviews the reconciliation should have an expectation of the date by which the monthly reconciliation review is due. "Lost" bank statements should be found or duplicates quickly requested from the bank.

Check Stock

Check Stock Log. A log document should record beginning and ending check numbers of check stock as ordered and received; such a log includes a continuously numbered record of check numbers issued and voided. The log can be linked to the counter of a signature plate, if used, and a record of checks manually issued and hand signed.

Controlled Access Storage. The company should create constantly locked storage for the check stock with dual access controls. Old-fashioned locks and keys still work, but new technologies for encryption or scanning personal features such as eyes or palm prints may be convenient. *Note:* The same type of security review can be applied to controls for access to documents or terminals used to effect wire transfers and record their authorization and occurrence.

The box of checks currently being used will, of course, be unsealed. Unopened boxes should be stored with the seals facing the storage area for easy visual verification that the boxes have not been opened. There should be random inventory reviews.

Control of Ordering Checks. The company management should determine who is authorized to order checks and to whose attention checks are delivered for entry into the controlled-access storage.

Check Stock Security.   Elaborate security features for check stock are available through check stock printing companies. Many companies, however, use inexpensive check stock with no counterfeiting protections. Yet however elaborate or simple the system, the first safeguard lies in selecting a color and paper so that an original is clearly distinguishable from a photocopy. Simple black printing on clear white paper is the least desirable and the most easy to use for scanned counterfeiting.

Unfortunately, anyone holding a company's check can order, through the Internet or from an unscrupulous printer, blank check stock with the same routing and transit and account numbers. The check stock may not match, but the company may not know that fraudulent checks are being paid through its account until it reconciles its bank statement (unless the company is protected by "positive pay," discussed in the next section).

A high-volume issuer of checks may seek more elaborate security features to deter would-be counterfeiters. In addition, a company issuing a high volume of payroll checks—instead of direct deposit items—may want unique check features that are recognized in the community of its employees, thus deterring payroll check counterfeiters. Direct deposit for payroll, of course, is likely to be much less expensive, as well as attractive from the point of view of fraud prevention.

The business entity issuing a low volume of checks with an ordinary appearance may be most vulnerable to fraudulent issuing or counterfeiting. Maintaining a low-balance checking account, funded only as checks are validly issued, may be a practical solution for this kind of entity.

Positive Pay Arrangements

A company's agreement with its bank for the provision of positive pay services is an extremely effective way to prevent certain types of fraud. In a typical positive pay arrangement, the company delivers a "check issue report" to the bank, listing by check number and amount all of the checks that were issued over a specified period, usually a banking day. As checks are presented to the bank, the bank compares each presented check with the information on the check issue report. If a check is presented that is not on the report or is shown differently in the report, the check is designated an "exception check."

A list of exception checks is sent to the company. Depending on the terms of the agreement between the bank and the company, the bank either pays the exception check—unless the company instructs the bank not to pay it—or returns the exception check—unless the company instructs the bank to pay it.

Positive pay procedures can detect unauthorized checks, checks bearing forged drawer's signatures, and checks that have been altered in amount. These procedures are highly recommended as a means of preventing fraud.

It is important to note, however, that a typical positive pay arrangement does not detect all types of check fraud. Most of the procedures utilized today capture the amount of the check and its number. They do not capture the payee's name or the writing on the back of the check. Thus, a typical positive pay procedure will not detect the alteration of the payee's name or a forged endorsement.

Warning: The company that signs a positive pay agreement should be wary, because such agreements often shift the liability for a fraudulent check from the bank to the customer when liability under the U.C.C. would otherwise have been allocated to the bank. A positive pay agreement, for example, may state:

> The Bank shall have no liability for a fraudulent check paid by the Bank in accordance with the procedures specified in this Agreement.

The foregoing provision would absolve the bank of liability for a check when the bank would otherwise have been liable for the check under the basic liability rules, such as for a check in which the payee's name has been altered. The positive pay procedures would typically not detect such a check, but the provision would shift liability for it from the bank to the customer. If the bank pays the check, the result is that signing the positive pay agreement has made the customer liable for a check for which the bank otherwise would have been liable—quite a perversion of the purpose of the positive pay agreement.

COMPANY THAT RECEIVES CHECKS

From the point of view of a company that is the recipient of a check, care must be taken to avoid the risks associated with the steps from receipt to deposit and, as noted earlier, from provisional to final settlement.

Receipt

Businesses receive checks by mail, and many businesses receive many checks at the **point of sale**.

Retail Point-of-Sale Receipts. Risk management procedures for retail point-of-sale receipts require an assessment of the degree of risk that the company is willing to accept. For example, many retail businesses use minimum procedures to verify checks for small amounts. Some retailers will accept any check that is preprinted and is drawn on a local bank by a drawer at a local address—although low-numbered checks drawn on new accounts may be selected for further scrutiny. Most retailers verify the identity of the drawer of the check with the information preprinted on the check.

Many retailers rely on validation services—most usually real-time electronic access—based on the identification of the check's drawer and the bank account information on the check. These services also provide alerts as to writers of bad checks and confirm that funds are probably available in the drawer's bank account. These validation services may offer some level of guarantee to the retailer and assume collection responsibility for unpaid items. Such services may be particularly useful for high-dollar-amount checks or at certain times of the year, such as around the December holidays.

Training those who accept point-of-sale checks to review the appearance of the magnetic ink character recognition (MICR) line on a check helps to intercept forged checks. The forger wants the check to "pass" at the point of sale and is not concerned whether it will "read" in the check processing systems. In many forgeries, the MICR line is incomplete or does not match the preprinted numbers at the top of the check.

A knowledge of the potential problems in regard to "holder in due course" can facilitate an understanding of why retailers rarely accept third-party checks (checks that have been endorsed to a third party). See the discussion of the holder in due course doctrine earlier in this chapter.

General Business Receipts. General business receipts are receipts outside the retail point-of-sale environment. These include checks from retail accounts not at the point of sale and the very large volume of business-to-business payments made by check.

A business expecting very large payments to be made by check, instead of by wire, may request payment by "certified check" or by official bank checks, sometimes called "bank drafts," "cashier's checks," or "teller's checks." In the discussion of drafts, it was explained how a certified check is an acceptance; the bank accepts the check, typically voiding the MICR so that the check will not process against its customer's account, stamping the check "Accepted" or "Certified," and adding the bank's identification number. Bank checks are checks for which the bank is both drawer and drawee—hence, "drawn on us" (the bank).

Ensuring that the checks received are all deposited to the company's account can be arranged by directing payments to a separate post office box with dual access control. Lockbox processing by a bank provides another method for this control.

Company That Receives Checks

Just as reviewing bank reconciliations is important to the issuer, reviewing accounts receivable is important to the receiver of checks. Reviewing "past due" accounts helps catch theft as well as improve cash flow. Payments that are posted to customer accounts but not deposited in the bank can be detected by preparing reconciliations of and comparing the totals on reports of change in accounts receivable to the total of bank deposits.

4

Wire Transfers: Originator to Its Bank to Receiving Bank

This chapter and the next discuss the links in the funds-transfer chain and highlight the many risk management opportunities. This chapter discusses a bank's right to decline to accept a customer's payment orders, requirements that a customer report fraudulent or erroneous transfers within specified periods following receipt of the bank statement, the liability of the bank and the customer for losses resulting from fraudulent payment orders, and interest that may be due to the customer from the bank. The discussion includes the bank's perspectives on the credit risks of the wire transfer payment system.

LINKS IN THE FUNDS-TRANSFER CHAIN

A **wire transfer transaction** is typically a series of instructions, called "payment orders." The sender of the first payment order is the "originator," and the first payment order is from the originator to the originator's bank. The ultimate recipient of the

59

funds transfer is the "beneficiary," and the last payment order is from the originator's bank or an intermediary bank to the beneficiary's bank. The series of payment orders may be viewed as "a funds-transfer chain," and each payment order as a "link" in the funds-transfer chain.

Thus, for example, if ABC Inc. wishes to send a wire transfer of $10,000 to XYZ Corp., ABC Inc. may originate the transfer by sending instructions to its bank, Bank A, to transfer $10,000 to XYZ Corp.'s account at Bank B. Bank A may execute ABC Inc.'s order by sending its own payment order to the Federal Reserve Bank in the region, instructing the Federal Reserve Bank to send funds to XYZ Corp.'s account at Bank C. The Federal Reserve Bank may then debit the account of Bank A for $10,000 and credit the account of Bank C for $10,000 and send instructions to Bank B that it has credited its account for the benefit of XYZ Corp.

In this example, ABC Inc. is the originator, Bank A is the originator's bank, the Federal Reserve Bank is an intermediary bank, Bank B is the beneficiary's bank, and XYZ Corp. is the beneficiary. The payment order from ABC Inc. to Bank A is the first link, the order from Bank A to the Federal Reserve Bank is the second link, and the order from the Federal Reserve Bank to Bank B is the third and last link in the funds-transfer chain. There can be any number of intermediary banks in a funds transfer, and thus any number of links in the chain.

Funds transfers are commonly called "wire transfers," but a payment order may be transmitted orally or in writing as well as electronically. Funds transfers are governed in each state of the United States by Article 4A of the Uniform Commercial Code (U.C.C.). Article 4A also applies to **book transfers**, also called **on-us transactions**, in which the originator and the beneficiary use the same bank. Article 4A generally does not apply to a transfer of funds into or out of the account of a consumer.

This chapter considers the first link, from the originator to the originator's bank, and subsequent links up to the last link in the chain. Chapter 5 considers the last link, the **payment order** to the beneficiary's bank.

Liability for fraud and liability for errors are two critical aspects of the relationships between the parties in a funds transfer. This chapter and the next discuss those relationships at each of the links in the funds-transfer chain.

Normally, the purpose of a funds transfer is to satisfy an obligation of the originator to the beneficiary. U.C.C. Article 4A dictates the point at which that obligation has been legally discharged.

Funds transfers are often for large amounts and are time sensitive for both the originating company and the beneficiary. It is important to understand what can go wrong—and the resulting responsibilities of the originating company and the banks—so as to be able to manage and mitigate the risks of fraud and errors.

ORIGINATOR AND ITS BANK

The originator's bank has no obligation to execute the originator's payment orders. The originator's bank can simply do nothing upon receipt of an order. If, however, the bank fails to execute an order when the originator's account contains available funds in an amount that is sufficient to cover the order, the bank may incur a limited obligation to pay interest to the originator. In addition to the passive right to do nothing at all upon the receipt of a payment order, the originator's bank has an active right to give notice of its rejection of the order. By giving such notice, the bank avoids incurring the interest obligation.

The originator may cancel or amend its payment order, but only if notice of the amendment or cancellation is received in a time and in a manner that affords the bank a reasonable opportunity to act on it. Once the payment order has been executed by the originator's bank, however, it cannot be canceled or amended except with the agreement of the bank.

If the bank accepts the originator's payment order by executing the order, the bank incurs the duty to comply with the instructions contained in the order. If it breaches that duty, it becomes liable to the originator, but its liability is limited to interest and interest losses, expenses in the funds transfer, and incidental expenses.

In addition to the bank's acceptance giving rise to a duty of the bank to comply with the originator's instructions, the bank's acceptance of the originator's payment order gives rise to an obligation of the originator to pay the originator's bank the amount of the originator's payment order. *Important:* The obligation of the originator to pay its bank is excused, however, if the funds transfer is not completed by the acceptance by the beneficiary's bank of a payment order instructing payment to the beneficiary of the originator's order.

The rules summarized in the preceding paragraphs are discussed in the following sections with an analysis of the resulting risks to the intended funds-transfer transaction.

Nonacceptance of Payment Orders

The receiving bank has both a passive right to take no action at all upon receiving a payment order and an affirmative right to reject the order by notice to the originator. By giving notice of rejection, the bank avoids incurring an interest obligation that it may otherwise incur for its failure to execute the order.

Bank's Passive Right Not to Execute Orders. U.C.C. Article 4A is very clear about the right of a bank to decline to execute a payment order. Unless the bank has become obligated to accept the order by an express agreement (such as a wire transfer agreement with the company) to do so, the receiving bank does not have

> any duty to accept a payment order or, before acceptance, to take any action, or refrain from taking any action, with respect to the order.[1]

> The payment order of the sender is treated under Article 4A as a request by the sender to the receiving bank to execute or pay the order and that request can be accepted or rejected by the receiving bank.[2]

Interest Penalty If the Bank Fails to Act or Notify.   If the receiving bank fails to take any action upon receipt of the payment order, however, the bank may incur an interest obligation to the originator. The interest obligation is incurred when the bank fails to execute the order, the sender has not received notice of rejection of the order on the execution date, and on the execution date there is a withdrawable credit balance in an authorized account of the sender sufficient to cover the order.[3] The execution date is the date on which the receiving bank may properly execute the order and is normally the day on which the order is received.[4] In addition, the interest obligation is incurred only if the account is not an interest-bearing account, and the period for which the interest is payable cannot exceed five funds-transfer business days after the execution date—and if the originator learns of the bank's failure to execute the order or receives notice of it prior to the expiration of the five-day period, the period terminates on that day.[5] The interest is payable at the Federal Funds Rate of the Federal Reserve Bank of New York unless the parties have agreed to a different rate of interest.[6]

Bank's Right to Reject Orders: Eliminate Interest Obligation

In addition to the passive right to ignore or do nothing at all upon its receipt of a payment order, a receiving bank has the right affirmatively to reject the payment order.[7] By exercising that right, the bank avoids the liability that it may otherwise have had to pay interest for its failure to execute the order.[8]

The notice of rejection may be sent orally, electronically, or in writing and need not use any particular words. The rejection is effective when the notice is given if the transmission is by a reasonable means. The originator and the originator's bank may agree upon the means of transmission. When they do so, the agreed-upon means is deemed reasonable, but note that the use of other means is not deemed unreasonable—unless a significant delay in receipt of the notice results.[9]

Rejected Funds-Transfer Request Risk Mitigation. It would be desirable, from the company's point of view, if its wire transfer agreement with the bank required the bank to give reasonably timely notice when the bank rejects a payment order. The bank, however, may be understandably reluctant to agree to be liable for significant damages for its failure to give such notice. In any case, the company should have procedures in place to ensure that it monitors its time-sensitive payment orders. If the company has an obligation to pay a certain amount by wire transfer on a certain date, it should not send the order to the bank and "go out to lunch for the rest of the day."

Cancellation and Amendment of Payment Orders

What if the sender makes a mistake—or a fraudulent transfer order is detected? Sometimes the sender of a payment order wants to cancel or amend the order. The Official Comments explain:

> The sender of a payment order may want to withdraw or change the order because the sender has had a change of mind about the transaction or because the payment order was erroneously issued or for any other reason. One common situation is that of multiple transmission of the same order. The sender that mistakenly transmits the same order twice wants to correct the mistake by cancelling the duplicate order. Or, a sender may have intended to order a payment of $1,000,000 but mistakenly issued an order to pay $10,000,000. In this case the sender might try to correct the mistake by cancelling the order and issuing another order in the proper amount. Or, the mistake could be corrected by amending the order to change it to the proper amount. Whether the error is corrected by amendment or cancellation and reissue the net result is the same.[10]

Article 4A allows the sender of a payment order to cancel or amend the order by communicating instructions to the bank to cancel or amend the order, provided that the communication is received "at a time and in a manner affording the bank a reasonable opportunity to act on the communication" *and before the bank has accepted the order.*[11]

Just as in the case of the original payment order, the instructions to cancel or amend the order may be transmitted orally, electronically, or in writing.[12] If a security procedure is in effect between the originator and the bank, the originator's communication is not effective unless it is verified pursuant to the security procedure or the bank agrees to the cancellation or amendment.[13]

Hurry! The originator is not likely to have much time in which to send effective cancellation or amendment instructions before the bank has accepted the payment order by executing it, that is, before the bank issues its own order to the next bank in the funds-transfer payment chain. After the bank has accepted the order, amendment or cancellation instructions are not effective unless the bank agrees to accept them.[14] If the bank has not yet accepted the order, the sender can unilaterally cancel or amend. The communication canceling or amending the payment order must be received in time to allow the bank to act on it before the bank issues its payment order in execution of the sender's order. The time that the sender's communication is received is defined by § 4A-106.[15] If a payment order does not specify a delayed payment date or execution date, the order will normally be executed shortly after receipt. Thus, as a practical matter, the sender will have very little time in which to instruct cancellation or amendment before acceptance. In addition, a receiving bank will normally have cutoff times for the receipt of such communications, and the receiving bank is not obliged to act on communications received after the cutoff time.[16]

Once the bank has accepted the originator's order by executing it, the payment order may not be canceled or amended except with the agreement of the receiving bank,[17] and even then the cancellation is not effective until the receiving bank has issued its own instructions canceling or amending the payment order it has issued to the next bank in the funds-transfer chain.[18]

The Official Comments explain why a bank that receives a cancellation request after it has executed the original payment order has no liability with respect to the request:

> Cancellation by the sender after execution of the order by the receiving bank requires the agreement of the bank unless a funds transfer rule otherwise provides.[19]

> Although execution of the sender's order by the receiving bank does not itself impose liability on the receiving bank (under Section 4A-402 no liability is incurred by the receiving bank to pay its order until it is accepted), it would commonly be the case that acceptance follows shortly after issuance. Thus as a practical matter, a receiving bank that has executed a payment order will incur a liability to the next bank in the chain before it would be able to act on the cancellation request of the customer. It is unreasonable to impose on the receiving bank a risk of loss with respect to a cancellation request without the consent of the receiving bank.[20]

Banks Affected by a Requested Amendment or Cancellation— Unraveling the Transfers.   If the originator is allowed to cancel its payment order, the entire transaction ought to be unraveled. "It makes no sense to allow cancellation of a payment order unless all subsequent payment orders in the funds transfer that were issued because of the canceled payment order are also canceled. Under [§ 4A-211(c)(1)], if a receiving bank consents to cancellation of the payment order after it is executed, the cancellation is not effective unless the receiving bank also cancels the payment order issued by the bank."[21] In other words, when the originator's order is canceled or amended after the originator's bank has executed the order, the funds transfer may be unraveled only with the consent of the parties that have participated in the transfer.

For example, suppose that the originator, intending to issue a payment order for $100,000, instead issues an order for $1,000,000 to its bank. The originator's bank executes the order by issuing its own order to an intermediary bank for $1,000,000. The originator asks its bank to agree to cancel the order. The originator's bank is not likely to agree to cancel the order unless it is certain that it will not be liable to the intermediary bank for the $1,000,000 order issued by the originator's bank. If the intermediary bank has executed the order by issuing its own payment order to the beneficiary's bank, the intermediary bank is not likely to agree to cancel the order without the agreement of the beneficiary's bank.

If the intermediary bank has not yet executed the payment order of the originator's bank, then the originator's bank and the intermediary bank can agree to unravel the transaction. Similarly, if the intermediary bank has executed the order but the beneficiary's bank has not yet accepted the payment order of the intermediary bank, then the three banks can agree to unravel the transaction under § 4A-211(c). Special rules apply when the beneficiary's bank has accepted the payment order and become obligated to pay the beneficiary.[22]

Risk Mitigation for the Customer. Careful review and dual controls can substantially reduce errors—"two sets of eyes are better than one." If the Company can quickly initiate wire transfers by computer terminal, the second set of eyes may be even more important to offset typographical errors or misreads of the computer printout.

Automatic Cancellation. Automatic cancellation of a payment order occurs when the order has not been accepted at the end of the fifth funds-transfer business day after the execution date or payment date of the order.[23] After the five-day period has expired, the payment order is considered to be "stale."

Payment orders normally are executed on the execution date or the day after. An order issued to the beneficiary's bank is normally accepted on the payment date or the day after. If a payment order is not accepted on its execution

67

or payment date or shortly thereafter, it is probable that there was some problem with the terms of the order or the sender did not have sufficient funds or credit to cover the amount of the order. U.C.C. Section 4A-211(d)] provides for cancellation by operation of law to prevent an unexpected delayed acceptance.[24]

Two More Rules about Cancellation.   First, after a payment order has been canceled, the order cannot be accepted.[25] (No going back and forth.) Second, a payment order is not revoked by the death or legal incapacity of the sender unless the bank knows of the death or of an adjudication of the sender's incapacity and has a reasonable opportunity to act before accepting the order.[26]

Acceptance and Execution of the Originator's Payment Order

The originator's bank "accepts" the originator's payment order by "executing" it, that is, by issuing its own payment order to an intermediary bank or the beneficiary's bank intended to carry out the payment order received by the originator's bank.[27]

Obligations of the Originating Bank.   When the originator's bank complies with a request and accepts the originator's order by executing it, the bank becomes obligated under § 4A-302(a) to issue, on the "execution date," its own payment order complying with the originator's instructions.

The execution date is the day on which the bank may properly issue its order, that is, the date on which the bank should execute the payment order in order to ensure that payment is made to the beneficiary when it is supposed to be made.[28] The originator's payment order may specify the execution date. If the date is not otherwise specified, the execution date is the date on which the originator's payment order is received—if it is received before the bank's stated cutoff hour for outgoing funds transfers. The originator's instructions may instead specify a "payment date," that is, the date on which the amount of the order is payable to the beneficiary at the beneficiary's bank. In that event, the execution date is the payment date or the earliest date thereafter on which execution is reasonably necessary in order to allow enough time for payment to the beneficiary on the payment date.

If the originator's bank accepts the originator's payment order by executing it, the bank's payment order to the next bank in the funds-transfer chain must comply with the originator's payment order, and the bank must follow the originator's instructions with respect to any intermediary bank or funds-transfer system to be used and with respect to the means of transmission of payment orders. *Comment on risk mitigation:* If the sender specifies the intermediary bank(s), the sender may lose the benefit of the "money-back guarantee" of Article 4A (see the following discussion).

If the sender's instructions state that the transfer is to be carried out telephonically, by wire transfer, or otherwise by the most expeditious means, the bank must transmit its payment order by the most expeditious means available and instruct any intermediary bank accordingly.[29]

The Official Comments explain the rules requiring the receiving bank to comply with the sender's instructions:

> Section 4A-302 states the manner in which the receiving bank may execute the sender's order if execution occurs. Subsection (1) states the residual rule. The payment order issued by the receiving bank must comply with the sender's order and, unless some other rule is stated in the section, the receiving bank is obliged to follow any instruction of the sender concerning which funds transfer system is to be used, which intermediary banks are to be used, and what means of transmission is to be used. The instruction of the sender may be incorporated in the payment order itself or may be given separately. For example, there may be a master agreement between the sender and receiving bank containing instructions governing payment orders to be issued from time to time by the sender

to the receiving bank. In most funds transfers, speed is a paramount consideration. A sender that wants assurance that the funds transfer will be expeditiously completed can specify the means to be used. The receiving bank can follow the instructions literally or it can use an equivalent means. For example, if the sender instructs the receiving bank to transmit by telex, the receiving bank could use telephone instead. [§ 4A-302(c).] In most cases the sender will not specify a particular means but will use a general term such as "by wire" or "wire transfer" or "as soon as possible." These words signify that the sender wants a same-day transfer. In these cases the receiving bank is required to use a telephonic or electronic communication to transmit its order and is also required to instruct any intermediary bank to which it issues its order to transmit by similar means. [§ 4A-302(a)(2).] In other cases, such as an automated clearing house transfer, a same-day transfer is not contemplated. Normally, the sender's instruction or the context in which the payment order is received makes clear the type of funds transfer that is appropriate. If the sender states a payment date with respect to the payment order, the receiving bank is obliged to execute the order at a time and in a manner to meet the payment date if that is feasible.[30]

Unless instructed to the contrary, the originator's bank may use any funds-transfer system, if the use of the system is reasonable, and may issue its payment order either directly to the beneficiary's bank or to an intermediary bank if the originator's order can be expeditiously carried out through the intermediary bank and the originator's bank exercises ordinary care in the selection of the intermediary bank.[31] The receiving bank is not required to follow the sender's instructions regarding a funds-transfer system if the bank determines in good faith that it is not feasible to follow the instructions or that doing so would unduly delay the completion of the transfer. The Official Comments explain the rules governing the selection of a funds-transfer system or intermediary bank:

> [Section 4A-302(b)] concerns the choice of intermediary banks to be used in completing the funds transfer, and the funds transfer system to be used. If the receiving bank is not instructed about the matter, it can issue an order directly to the beneficiary's bank or can issue an order to an intermediary bank. The receiving bank also has discretion concerning use of a funds transfer system. In some cases it is reasonable to use either an automated clearing house system or a wire transfer system such as Fedwire or CHIPS. Normally, the receiving bank will follow the instruction of the sender in these matters, but in some cases it may be prudent for the bank not to follow instructions. The sender may have designated a funds transfer system to be used in carrying out the funds transfer, but it may not be feasible to use the designated system because of some impediment such as a computer breakdown which prevents prompt execution of the order. The receiving bank is permitted to use an alternative means of transmittal in a good faith effort to execute the order expeditiously. The same leeway is not given to the receiving bank if the sender designates an intermediary bank through which the funds transfer is to be routed. The sender's designation of that intermediary bank may mean that the beneficiary's bank is expecting to obtain a credit from the intermediary bank and may have relied on that anticipated credit. If the receiving bank uses another intermediary bank the expectations of the beneficiary's bank may not be realized. The receiving bank could choose to route the transfer to another intermediary bank and then to the designated intermediary bank if there were some reason such as a lack of a correspondent-bank relationship or a bilateral credit limitation, but the designated intermediary bank cannot be circumvented. To do so violates the sender's instruction.[32]

Funds-Transfer Charges. Suppose the originator's bank uses an intermediary bank and the intermediary bank deducts its charges from the amount of the payment order it sends to the beneficiary's bank. The beneficiary will be deprived of the full payment of the originator's order. This problem is addressed in § 4A-302(d). The receiving bank may not on its own deduct its charges from the amount of the payment order it issues in execution of the sender's orders or instruct subsequent banks in the funds-transfer chain to do so. However, it may deduct the charges or instruct a subsequent receiving bank to deduct the charges if the sender has authorized the receiving bank to do so.[33] The Official Comments explain the problem of a bank's deducting charges from the point of view of the beneficiary:

> In some cases, particularly if it is an intermediary bank that is executing an order, charges are collected by deducting them from the amount of the payment order issued by the executing bank. If that is done, the amount of the payment order accepted by the beneficiary's bank will be slightly less than the amount of the originator's payment order. . . . Subsection (d) of Section 4A-302 allows Intermediary Bank to collect its charges by deducting them from the amount of the payment order, but only if instructed to do so by Originator's Bank. Originator's Bank is not authorized to give that instruction to Intermediary Bank unless Originator authorized the instruction. Thus Originator can control how the charges of Originator's Bank and Intermediary Bank are to be paid.[34]

For example, an intermediary bank deducts a $25 funds-transfer charge from the amount of the payment order sent to the Beneficiary's Bank, with or without the authorization of the Originator. The $1,000,000 funds-transfer payment was to preserve valuable option rights, and the Beneficiary asserts that because of the deduction, the Originator has lost the option rights.

Section 4A-405(c) rescues the Originator. If the beneficiary's bank accepts a payment order in an amount that is equal to the originator's order *less the charges of one or more receiving banks in the funds-transfer chain,* the beneficiary is deemed to have been paid the full amount of the originator's order unless the beneficiary demands that the originator pay the deducted charges and the originator fails to honor the demand.

Liability of the Bank for Breach of Its Funds-Transfer Obligations. The liability of the bank for breaching its obligations to the originator under § 4A-302 is governed by § 4A-305. Section 4A-305 covers "improper" execution. If funds have been erroneously transferred out of the originator's account, the bank may be liable to the originator for "erroneous" execution as well. Improper execution occurs under § 4A-305 when the bank's breach of its § 4A-302 obligations results in:

- A delay in the payment to the beneficiary,
- The noncompletion of the funds transfer,
- The failure to use an intermediary bank designated by the originator, or
- The issuance of a payment order that does not comply with the terms of the originator's payment order.

Improper execution also occurs when the bank fails to execute a payment order that it was obliged to execute by express agreement.

Because the drafters of Article 4A wanted to maintain the low cost of wire transfers, the bank's liability for improper execution under § 4A-305 is severely limited. Indeed, although it is true that § 4A-305 imposes liability on the receiving bank for improper execution of the sender's payment orders, it also, which is just as important, limits the liability of the bank for improper execution to interest and funds transfer and incidental expenses. From the point of view of the originator, the true significance of these provisions is that the originator must monitor its important funds transfers. If an important transfer is delayed or goes awry, the originator will have no right of recovery from the bank other than a nominal amount.

If the breach results in the delay of payment to the beneficiary, the bank is obligated to pay interest to either the originator or the beneficiary for the period of delay caused by the breach.[35] The Official Comments explain:

> With respect to wire transfers (other than ACH [automated clearing house] transactions) within the United States, the expectation is that the funds transfer will be completed on the same day. In those cases, the originator can reasonably expect that the originator's account will be debited on the same day as the beneficiary's account is credited. If the funds transfer is delayed, compensation can be paid either to the originator or [to] the beneficiary. The normal practice is to compensate the beneficiary's bank to allow that bank to compensate the beneficiary by back-valuing the payment by the number of days of delay. Thus, the beneficiary is in the same position that it would have been in if the funds transfer had been completed on the same day. Assume on Day 1, Originator's Bank issues its payment order to Intermediary Bank which is received on that day. Intermediary Bank does not execute that order until Day 2 when it issues an order to Beneficiary's Bank which is accepted on that day. Intermediary Bank complies with [§ 4A-305(a)] by paying one day's interest to Beneficiary's Bank for the account of Beneficiary.[36]

If the improper execution results in the noncompletion of the funds transfer,[37] the failure to use an intermediary bank designated by the originator, or issuance of a payment order that does not comply with the terms of the originator's payment order, the bank is liable to the originator for the originator's expenses in the funds transfer, the originator's incidental expense[38] and interest losses, and interest.[39]

Except for attorney's fees, discussed later in this section, no other amounts are recoverable by the originator for the bank's improper execution of the originator's payment order except to the extent that the bank has expressly agreed in writing to pay such additional amounts.[40]

The principal effect of the § 4A-305 provisions governing liability for improper execution is to eliminate the bank's exposure to "consequential damages"—damages that would not normally be foreseeable. Under traditional common law principles, such damages are not recoverable by the aggrieved party (the party that has been damaged by the other party's breach of its obligations) from the culpable party (the party that has breached its obligations). However, when the culpable party has been put on notice of the special circumstances that give rise to the consequential damages, the damages become recoverable from the culpable party.[41]

Section 4A-305(c) makes clear that only the damages specified in § 4A-305—incidental expenses, expenses in the funds transfer, and interest losses—are recoverable for a bank's breach of its § 4A-302 obligations. Other damages, including consequential damages, are not recoverable *unless the bank has expressly agreed in writing to pay them*—even when the bank has been given notice of special circumstances that will give rise to the consequential damages that would result from the bank's breach of its § 4A-302 obligations.

The Official Comments discuss the Article 4A rule on consequential damages.

> In the typical case, transmission of the payment order is made electronically. Personnel of the receiving bank that process payment orders are not the appropriate people to evaluate the risk of liability for consequential damages in relation to the price charged for the wire transfer service. Even if notice is received by higher level management personnel who could make an appropriate decision whether the risk is justified by the price, liability based on

notice would require evaluation of payment orders on an individual basis. This kind of evaluation is inconsistent with the high-speed, low-price, mechanical nature of the processing system that characterizes wire transfers. . . . The success of the wholesale wire transfer industry has largely been based on its ability to effect payment at low cost and great speed. Both of these essential aspects of the modern wire transfer system would be adversely affected by a rule that imposed on banks liability for consequential damages.[42]

Suppose the originator and the originator's bank have signed an agreement in which the bank agrees that it will execute the customer's payment orders. Are consequential damages recoverable if the bank breaches that obligation? No, the damages recoverable under § 4A-305 for the bank's breach of an express agreement to execute a payment order are virtually the same as if there were no agreement. The sender may recover only its expenses in the transaction and its incidental expenses and interest losses resulting from the bank's failure to execute the order. However, additional damages are recoverable, including consequential damages, if the bank has expressly agreed in writing to pay the additional damages.[43] The bank would be liable, for example, for tax penalties if it has agreed to pay the penalties resulting from its late execution of a funds transfer to a tax collection agency.

In addition to interest expenses and losses and incidental expenses and expenses incurred in the funds-transfer transaction, attorney's fees may be recovered from the receiving bank when the bank's breach results in a delay in payment to the beneficiary under § 4A-305(a) or in noncompletion, failure to use a designated intermediary bank, or issuance of a noncomplying payment order under § 4A-305(b). The fees are recoverable, however, only if demand for compensation is made and refused before suit is brought against the receiving bank.[44]

Attorney's fees are similarly recoverable when the bank has breached an express written agreement to execute the payment order under § 4A-305(d) but not if the agreement provides for damages for the breach. The reason given for this rule, that attorney's fees are not available when the agreement provides for damages, is that the damages agreed upon by the parties "may or may not provide for attorney's fees."[45]

Notes to Negotiators of Wire Transfer Agreements.[46] Negotiators should be aware of the following:

1. *The bank's liability for interest expense, expenses in the funds transaction, incidental expenses, and interest losses under § 4A-305 may not be disclaimed by the bank by agreement. Negotiators for the customer should resist provisions that purport to disclaim such liability.*[47]

2. *If funds transfers are for a specific purpose, the agreement can provide that the bank will be liable for improper execution or failure to execute payment orders when that purpose is frustrated.* Thus, the bank can agree to be liable for tax penalties when it improperly executes or fails to execute a payment to a tax collection agency or liable for foreign exchange losses when the transfer is to sell or purchase foreign currency.

"Money-Back Guarantee"

The sender of a payment order is obliged to pay the receiving bank the amount of the order when the receiving bank accepts the order. Thus, if the originator's bank accepts the originator's order by executing it, the originator becomes obligated to pay the originator's bank the amount of the order—even though the payment is not due until the execution date of the order.[48]

If the funds transfer is not completed by acceptance by the beneficiary's bank of a payment order instructing payment to the beneficiary of the sender's order, the obligation of the sender to pay for the order is excused. If the sender has already paid for the payment order, the sender is entitled to a refund under § 4A-402(d). These provisions are described in the Official Comments as a "money-back guarantee."[49]

Money-Back Guarantee Risk Mitigation for the Originating Company. The originator is assured that it will not lose its money if something goes wrong in the transfer. For example, risk of loss resulting from payment to the wrong beneficiary is borne by the bank, not by the originator. The most likely reason for noncompletion is a failure to execute or an erroneous execution of a payment order by the bank originating the funds transfer or by an intermediary bank. The sending bank may have issued its payment order to the wrong bank, or it may have identified the wrong beneficiary in its order. The money-back guarantee is particularly important to the originator if noncompletion of the funds transfer is the fault of an intermediary bank. In that case, the company's bank has the burden of obtaining a refund from the intermediary bank that it paid.[50]

Thus, for example, if the originator issues a payment order to its bank, the originator's bank issues its order to an intermediary bank, and the intermediary bank erroneously executes the order by sending the funds to the wrong bank, the money-back guarantee assures the originator that it is excused from the obligation to pay its bank. If the originator's bank has already been paid, the bank will have to refund the amount of the order to the originator. The remedy of the originator's bank would be to seek reimbursement from the intermediary bank.

Exception to the Money-Back Guarantee. There is an exception to the money-back guarantee. The intermediary bank may have encountered solvency problems. If the originator instructed the originator's bank to route the payment order to that particular intermediary bank, then the originator loses the benefits of the money-back guarantee; the originator's bank would be entitled to payment from the originator, and the originator's remedy is to seek reimbursement from the intermediary bank.[51]

Statute of Repose

Sender's Right to Refund Expires. When a customer of the bank has paid the bank for a payment order issued in the customer's name that has been accepted by the bank, and the customer has received notice of the order, the customer cannot wait indefinitely to object to the transfer. The customer's objection may be a valid one—for example, that the transfer was fraudulent or erroneously executed—but the customer cannot "sleep on its rights."

The customer must assert its objection within one year after receiving the notice. If the customer waits until after the year has expired, the customer is precluded from asserting the objection. The purpose of the provision is to prevent the assertion of stale claims.

> The soothing word "repose" suggests tranquility and rest, and the provision embodies the principle that an issue should be "put to rest" and dispute foreclosed when no dispute concerning the matter has arisen after the passage of a very long time.
>
> If funds have been transferred fraudulently, or to the wrong person, or in an excessive amount, recovery of the funds is likely to become more difficult over the passage of time. The Statute of Repose penalizes the customer who waits one year after objecting to a funds transfer by depriving the customer of the right to object to it.[52]

Funds-Transfer Agreement Negotiating Point. A very significant question is whether the one-year period under the Statute of Repose may be reduced to a lesser period by the agreement of the parties. The answer to that question would at first blush appear to be yes, that the one-year period may be reduced. The general rule for variation of the rules of Article 4A is that the parties by agreement may vary the rules except as otherwise provided in Article 4A.[53]

Certainly, there is no provision in Article 4A that prevents the bank from varying the one-year period under the Statute of Repose and requiring the customer to assert objections to transfers sooner than the expiration of the one-year period. However, the effect of enforcing that requirement may be to shift liability to the customer under circumstances in which:

- The bank would otherwise be liable for the loss, and
- The bank is not permitted under Article 4A to disclaim its liability.

Suppose, for example, that the funds-transfer agreement requires the customer to report fraudulent transfers within 30 days of receipt of notice of the transfer. The bank receives a fraudulent payment order and pays the order without verifying the authenticity of the order in accordance with the security procedure it has agreed to use for that purpose. Because the bank has failed to use the security procedure to verify the order, the bank is liable for the loss.[54] Moreover, the bank's liability is not variable, that is, the bank may not by agreement disclaim its liability for the loss.[55]

Suppose, however, that the customer has failed to comply with a requirement in the funds-transfer agreement that it report fraudulent transfers within 30 days of receipt of notice of the transfer. If the bank can enforce that agreement against the customer and thereby avoid liability for the loss, then the bank has *varied* a *nonvariable provision* of Article 4A. In other words, the bank has avoided liability for its failure to verify the authenticity of the payment order, even though the bank is not permitted to disclaim that liability under Article 4A.

Thus, it is not clear whether the 30-day reporting requirement in the example is a permissible reduction of the one-year period under the Statute of Repose or an impermissible attempt to avoid liability that the bank may not avoid under the nonvariable provisions that impose liability on the bank for fraud when the bank has failed to use the security procedure to verify the authenticity of a fraudulent payment order.

Funds-transfer agreements typically contain provisions that reduce the Statute of Repose, sometimes to very brief periods—such as 5 days—or, more commonly, to periods such as 30 days. It may seem reasonable to the customer's negotiator that the customer should reconcile its bank statements within, say, 30 days, but the negotiator must be mindful that the consequences of agreeing to do so may be to shift the liability for a fraudulent transfer to the customer, or shift liability to refund an errant transfer under the "money-back guarantee," when Article 4A dictates not only that the bank is liable for the transfer, but also that the bank cannot disclaim that liability.

The customer is thus advised to be extremely wary of provisions in its funds-transfer agreement that require the customer to report fraudulent or erroneous transfers within a specified period after receipt of the customer's bank statement.[56]

LIABILITY FOR FRAUDULENT FUNDS TRANSFERS

Under the basic rule allocating liability for a fraudulent transfer between the bank and the customer, the customer is liable for the resulting loss, provided that the bank and the customer have agreed upon a security procedure to verify the authenticity of the customer's payment orders and:

- The security procedure is a commercially reasonable procedure,
- The bank proves that it accepted the payment order in compliance with the security procedure and with the customer's written instructions, and
- The bank proves that it accepted the payment order in good faith.

Thus, in a garden-variety fraud case, the customer will be liable for the loss if the bank utilized a security procedure to verify that the payment order was an authentic order of the customer and the procedure was a "commercially reasonable" procedure. In deciding whether the security procedure was a commercially reasonable one, Article 4A instructs the court to consider the wishes and circumstances of the customer, including the size, type, and frequency of payment orders normally issued by the customer, to consider alternative security procedures offered to the customer, and to consider security procedures in general use by customers and banks similarly situated.

If the customer objects to the use of the procedure offered by the bank on the grounds that the procedure is expensive or cumbersome or for any other reason, the bank may avoid liability even if the procedure selected by the customer is not commercially reasonable, provided that the customer expressly agrees in writing to be bound by payment orders accepted by the bank in compliance with the chosen procedure.

There is an important exception to the rule allocating liability to the bank when the bank has used a commercially reasonable security procedure. The exception relates to "interlopers." An interloper is a person not associated with the customer as specified in U.C.C. Article 4. More particularly, an interloper is a person who:

- Is not entrusted with duties to act for the customer relating to payment orders or the security procedure, or
- Has not obtained access to transmitting facilities of the customer or information facilitating a breach of the security procedure from a source controlled by the customer.

If the customer can prove that the wrongdoer was an interloper, then under the exception to the basic rule, the bank is liable for the loss resulting from the fraud.

Notes for Negotiators of Funds-Transfer Agreements

When negotiating funds-transfer agreements with the bank, the following are two key points to remember.

First, the standard forms of agreements used by banks often contain provisions that would impose liability on the customer when the bank would otherwise be liable under U.C.C. Article

4A. For example, an agreement might provide as follows: "The bank will not be liable for its acceptance of any payment order under this Agreement unless the bank's conduct has constituted gross negligence or willful misconduct" or "The bank will not be liable for having accepted any payment order the bank reasonably believes to have been that of the customer." U.C.C. Article 4A forbids the use of such provisions. Although they may be unenforceable, the customer should resist them.

Second, it is generally not in the best interests of the customer to decline a security procedure offered by the bank in favor of a procedure that the customer believes to be less cumbersome or one that is less expensive. The customer should be wary of provisions in the agreement that seem to state that the customer has agreed to use a security procedure that may not be commercially reasonable when the customer has not knowingly done so.

Liability for Misdescription of the Beneficiary

The originator may describe the beneficiary by both name and account number. For example, the originator may instruct the bank to pay John Doe, account number 12345 at Big Bank. If John Doe's account number is actually 12340, the rules for errors apply. See the discussion under "Rules for Errors" in Chapter 5.

Interest

Article 4A provides that when interest is due from the bank to the customer, the rate applicable is the Federal Funds Rate as published by the Federal Reserve Bank of New York. If the bank refunds the amount of the payment order because the transfer was not completed, and the failure to complete the transfer was not due to any fault of the bank, the rate of compensation is reduced by the applicable reserve requirement of the bank. If the bank is liable for interest compensation because it has failed to give notice of its rejection of a payment order, the customer's right to compensation is terminated five days after the execution date of the order.

The customer may seek to alter these provisions in the funds-transfer agreement. For example, to the extent that the reason for awarding interest is restitution to the customer for the use of the customer's funds, the customer may argue that the rate it pays for overnight funds is a more appropriate rate than the Federal Funds Rate.

NEXT LINK IN THE FUNDS-TRANSFER CHAIN: SENDING AND RECEIVING BANKS

Now the next link in the funds-transfer chain is considered—the relationship between banks and how it affects the risks of the originating company and its intended beneficiary company.

If the originator's bank executes the originator's payment order, the bank sends its own payment order to another bank, either an intermediary bank or the beneficiary's bank. In this second link, the originator's bank is a sender and the bank that accepts the payment order of the originator's bank is a receiving bank.

Most of the rules that apply to the originator's bank as a sender in this second link are stated in Article 4A to be applicable to the "sender" and not solely to the originator's bank. As a result, the rules that govern the rights and obligations of the originator as a sender generally apply as well to the originator's bank as a sender. Similarly, the rules that apply to the originator's bank as the receiving bank in the first link generally apply as well to the receiving bank in the second link.

For example, just as the originator's bank has full freedom to decline to accept the originator's payment order, the second bank in the funds-transfer chain is also free to decline to accept the payment order of the originator's bank.[57] Just as the originator's bank accepts the originator's payment order by executing it, that is, by issuing its own payment order to the next bank in the funds-transfer chain, so does an intermediary bank accept the payment order of the originator's bank by similarly executing it.[58]

The intermediary bank that accepts the payment order of the originator's bank is obliged to comply with the sender's payment order, just as the originator's bank was obliged to do;[59] and if the intermediary bank breaches that obligation, the bank is obliged to pay interest, interest losses, the sender's expenses in the funds transfer, and the sender's incidental expenses, but not consequential damages, all as described with respect to the originator and the originator's bank in the preceding section.[60]

When the intermediary bank accepts the payment order of the originator's bank, the originator's bank becomes obligated to pay the amount of its payment order,[61] but the "money-back guarantee" provisions protect the originator's bank as a sender just as they protect the originator. If the funds transfer is not completed, each bank in the funds-transfer chain leading to the beneficiary's bank is excused from its obligation to pay its order and is entitled to a refund if it has already paid for the order.[62]

If the money-back guarantee does not apply and a sending bank becomes obligated to pay its payment order to the receiving bank, how is payment or settlement achieved?[63] The originator's bank and the intermediary bank or beneficiary's bank may send and receive funds transfers between each other, either on a one-to-one basis or as part of a network. The amount of each payment order sent and received may be debited or credited to the account of one bank at the other bank or debited or credited to a clearing house account. The debits or credits may be netted against each other, and the net debit may be settled through a Federal Reserve account, charging the account of the net debtor and crediting the amount of the net creditor. In a Fedwire funds transfer, the obligation of the sending bank to pay its payment order is always settled by a debit to the account of the sending bank and a credit to the account of the receiving bank.

Any such settlement through the Federal Reserve system, a funds-transfer system, or payment by netting constitutes payment of the sender's obligation to pay its payment order under Article 4A.[64] By making clear that the obligations of any sending bank are netted against the obligations of receiving banks to the sending bank, the net liability of the sending bank is reduced, thereby reducing the risk in the event of the insolvency of the sending bank.[65]

If the receiving bank credits the account of the sending bank or causes the sending bank's account at another bank to be credited, payment of the sender's obligation to pay its payment order occurs when the credit is withdrawn (or at midnight of the day on which the credit is withdrawable and the receiving bank learns that it is withdrawable).[66] If the receiving bank debits the account of the sending bank and the debit is covered by a withdrawable credit balance, the debit constitutes payment.[67]

Originating Company's Money-Back Guarantee

The originating company is entitled to the benefit of its money-back guarantee regardless of the logistics between its bank and a subsequent receiving bank(s).

MANAGING RISKS IN THE LINKS OF THE WIRE TRANSFER PAYMENT SYSTEM

Originator and Its Bank

A company should have a written agreement with its bank for the bank to accept and execute the company's wire transfer payment orders.

The agreement should not allow the bank to shift its legal liabilities back to the company by short-period reporting requirements. See the discussion in this chapter about Negotiating Funds Transfer Agreements and in Chapter 8 about Contractual Risk Allocation. For example, a company should be wary of a provision that states, "Customer shall notify Bank within ___ days after receipt of the periodic statement of an alleged fraudulent or erroneous item."

The personnel of the company responsible for sending wire transfers should carefully check the wire transfer instructions before sending a wire. Once it is sent to the bank, canceling or amending the payment order is very difficult. The company needs the bank's written agreement that it has canceled or amended a payment order.

Some companies use dual control for review of nonrecurring wire transfer instructions. For recurring wire transfers, preformatted wire transfer orders are very helpful in reducing errors, because all of the data required do not have to be reentered for each transaction.

Computer terminal printouts and screen data can appear very quickly. Personnel responsible for sending wire transfers should carefully verify computer data. Dual control can help reduce errors. The process of signing the internal record of a payment order prior to releasing the payment order to the bank may slow the process sufficiently to reduce inadvertent errors.

The company should use the reporting services from its bank to verify that its payment orders have been executed. Most reporting is available on the same day or by the beginning of the next business day.

The company should promptly review and verify with its records all bank notices and bank statements. All notices to the bank about questions or errors should be in writing, and the bank's receipt of the notice verified. Find the name of the department or person to whom notices should be addressed.

Sending and Receiving Banks

The originator should carefully consider the risk of specifying intermediary banks for its wire transfer payment orders. See the discussion in this chapter about Money-Back Guarantee so the company does not lose this benefit. The circumstances for an originator to name the intermediary bank are unusual.

Important: The risks of the wire transfer payment system are best controlled before a wire transfer order is released by the company to its bank. Preventing errors and fraud are very difficult thereafter.

STUDY OF A BANK'S PERSPECTIVE OF FUNDS-TRANSFER RISK MANAGEMENT: WIRE TRANSFER SYSTEMS LEND MONEY TO CUSTOMERS

From the perspective of the bank, wire transfer systems "lend money" to their customers. How does this happen? How can systems be designed to reduce the inherent credit risk of such a loan?

Why Do Banks "Lend" Money for Transfers? Intra-Day Loans

There are three reasons that banks "lend" money for transfers:

1. *Timing.* Commercial wire transfers involve the movement of huge amounts of money from one place to another. This movement creates funding gaps for customers when the orders to transfer funds arrive before "the cover," the funds covering the outgoing transfer requests. This leads to the bank's first dilemma—to pay or to wait.

2. *Volume.* This decision—whether to pay or to wait—would be easy if volumes were small, but customers often have dozens of transfers in flight at the same time. Waiting to match each transfer with its intended cover payment is just not practical. Wire transfer systems handle the work of hundreds and sometimes thousands of customers at the same time. They are also trying simultaneously to control the bank's own position with settlement and clearing facilities. This makes transfer-to-cover matching even more impractical—not impossible, just impractical.

3. *Service.* With today's technology, systems could be built to deal with these issues and avoid all intra-day borrowings, *but service would suffer.*[68] One of the most critical ways in which large banks compete with each other for institutional payments business is by making it easy for customers to move these enormous sums, and this means taking some risk. Customers make good use of this service by targeting just the right amount of cover at just the right time at just the right place.

Controlling these intra-day loans, also known as "daylight overdrafts," is the primary risk management requirement for a wire transfer system.

What Is the Business Process Behind Daylight Overdrafts?

The most obvious risk with **daylight overdrafts** is that the money is not repaid. Banks protect themselves from this by developing policies that address the establishment, administration, and application of overdrafts.

The first question is, "How much?" Certainly, an Exxon or a General Motors can justify more daylight overdraft than a small local business, but how much more? How much is safe, even for a large corporation? Should this overdraft be considered in conjunction with other limits, such as the credit limit for loans? How much weight should be given to one kind of risk versus another, and how does this weighting affect operational limits?

In most instances, the Daylight Overdraft Limits (DOL) given to large, healthy institutions will be as generous as necessary to make transfer operations work smoothly. This is because it is rare for large corporations, brokers, banks, insurance companies, governments, and others of such entities to go out of business or default on legitimate claims in the middle of the day without some prior warning. But surprises, although rare, do happen, and given the huge amounts of money[69] involved, the loss potential is significant.

Another interesting consideration is that different kinds of payments have different settlement risks. Payments made to a clearing house, such as the New York Clearing House (NYCH), for example, are "insured" to some degree by the rules of the association (whereby the members agree to share in a loss caused by certain inabilities to settle—for example, with Clearing House Interbank Payment System (CHIPS) Rule 13). Payments made to a foreign correspondent bank, on the other hand, typically offer no assurance of settlement other than the foreign bank's agreement to settle the debts associated with its account. Should this difference in the level of safety be passed on to the customer in its DOL? That is, should there be a different DOL for each payment method?

For most banks, the answer is a resounding *no*. It is simply too difficult to administer and track multiple kinds of DOLs in a real-world situation. Accordingly, the DOL established for a customer reflects a blended level of safety for all payment mechanisms.

Because each customer using the wire transfer service will have one and only one DOL, the calculation used during the day to determine whether a requested payment should be made is:

Opening account balance + money received today – money paid out today + DOL = Payment amount

Wire transfer systems typically receive a balance update at the start of the business day from the bank's overnight demand deposit accounting (DDA) system. The DOL information is maintained as part of the funds-transfer system's static database, the monies in and out are the sum of the transfers in and the transfers out maintained by the transfer system, and the requested payment amount is the amount to be transferred.

In addition to the balance-oriented DOL, banks establish a transaction limit for each customer. The transaction limit reflects the "typical maximum" transfer amount made by the customer. Although customers occasionally exceed this transfer amount limit, it does provide another level of risk protection. The check here is simple:

Payment amount limit = Payment amount

These two checks represent the most basic risk management controls and are found in every wire transfer system.

Coping with Corporate Groups

Wire transfer customers are often members of larger groups that have their own risks. For example, all the customers in a particular country or region, or all the "accounts" associated with a particular corporation, bank, or government can constitute a group. Softer associations, such as an industry, can also be defined as groups worthy of daylight overdraft risk management. Typically, only the most sophisticated or custom-built wire transfer systems have the capability to deal with the risks inherent in groups.

Defining a "Customer." The first difficultly in addressing groups is to accurately define a "customer." Customers are really parties that play certain roles. In the fund-transfer process, these roles can be those of "instructor," "sender," "order party," "beneficiary," "pay through bank," and so forth. For risk management purposes, the most important roles are those in which the party has legal rights and responsibilities. For example, the entity that opens an account and signs the account agreement must be a legal entity. Such legal entities establish a legal relationship with the bank, which is also a legal entity that is defined by specific terms and conditions.

In comparison, an "office" of a corporation being advised about the receipt of funds does not have to be a legal entity. It does, however, need an address for receiving advising notices. The "instructor" of the funds transfer also does not have to be a legal entity. Such a person does, however, need to be empowered with the appropriate permissions by a legal entity.

Because of this special legal relationship, legal entities are the focus of risk management and, in effect, are the "customers" for this purpose. For the same reason, even though they are not legal entities themselves, groups must be composed of legal entities for risk management purposes. Accordingly, banks issue DOLs for individual legal entities (account owners) and for groups of legal entities.

Examples. Suppose Corporation X has five Divisions (X1 through X5). Each Division is itself a legal entity and each opens an account with Bank Y. To facilitate the large number of payments that will flow through each Division's account, the bank sets up for each Division an overdraft limit of $1 billion. It wants to ensure, however, that the total daylight overdraft for Corporation X does not exceed $3 billion.

Bank Y also sets a transaction limit of $5 million to $10 million for each Division and a transaction limit of $10 million for Corporation X as a whole. This arrangement can be seen in Exhibit 4.1.

The algorithms necessary to control transfers are illustrated in Exhibit 4.2.

A variation on this example is that the DOL desired for Corporation X is the sum of the DOLs assigned to each Division (the $5 billion). This can be seen in Exhibit 4.3.

It is important to note that in both examples, Corporation X does not itself have an account with Bank Y; instead, it simply designates the group. If there were an account for Corporation X, and if that account were specifically designated as part of this group, it would appear as it does in Exhibit 4.4.

The purpose of all of these arrangements is to provide another level of risk management control over the funds-transfer process. Requested funds transfers that exceed these limits are not automatically returned, but are instead earmarked for further scrutiny and approval.

Exhibit 4.1 Daylight Overdraft Limits (DOL) and Transaction Limits for Divisions That Are Legal Entities and Account Holders of a Corporation; DOL Corporation Total Is Less Than Sum of Entities' DOL

	Legal Entity/ Account Holder	DOL	Transaction Limit
Division X1	Yes/Yes	1,000,000,000	5,000,000
Division X1	Yes/Yes	1,000,000,000	10,000,000
Division X1	Yes/Yes	1,000,000,000	8,000,000
Division X1	Yes/Yes	1,000,000,000	9,000,000
Division X1	Yes/Yes	1,000,000,000	5,000,000
Corporation X	Yes/No	3,000,000,000	10,000,000

Exhibit 4.2 Algorithms to Central Transfers for Entities in Exhibit 4.1

Is the Account's...	Is the Group's...	Then	Is the Account's...	Is the Group's...	Then
Opening Balance +Money received −Money sent +DOL >payment amount?	Opening Balance +Money received −Money sent +DOL >payment amount?		Transaction limit >payment amount?	Transaction limit >payment amount?	
Yes	Yes	Test Txn limit	Yes	Yes	Pay
No	Yes	Test Txn limit	No	Yes	Pay
Yes	No	Reject	Yes	No	Reject
No	No	Reject	No	No	Reject

Exhibit 4.3 Variation of Exhibit 4.1; DOL Total Equals Sum of DOL for All Entities

	Legal Entity/ Account Holder	DOL	Transaction Limit
Division X1	Yes/Yes	1,000,000,000	5,000,000
Division X1	Yes/Yes	1,000,000,000	10,000,000
Division X1	Yes/Yes	1,000,000,000	8,000,000
Division X1	Yes/Yes	1,000,000,000	9,000,000
Division X1	Yes/Yes	1,000,000,000	5,000,000
Corporation X	Yes/No	5,000,000,000	10,000,000

Exhibit 4.4 Variation with Parent Corporation Also an Account Holder

	Legal Entity/ Account Holder	DOL	Transaction Limit
Division X1	Yes/Yes	1,000,000,000	5,000,000
Division X1	Yes/Yes	1,000,000,000	10,000,000
Division X1	Yes/Yes	1,000,000,000	8,000,000
Division X1	Yes/Yes	1,000,000,000	9,000,000
Division X1	Yes/Yes	1,000,000,000	5,000,000
Corporation X	Yes/Yes	1,000,000,000	10,000,000
Corporation X Group	No/No	6,000,000,000	

Handling Rejects

Transfers that are "rejected" because of DOL and/or violation of Transaction Limit must be:

- Approved or rejected by an authorized individual,
- Placed in a hold state, or
- Resubmitted for a new balance check (to see if more money has entered the account).

When are these actions performed? How are transfer queue priorities established? How are delays and/or handling errors avoided? These questions may sound arcane, but they are of vital interest when millions or even billions of dollars are involved.

When a transfer is rejected because of inadequate balance + DOL or for exceeding the Transaction Limit, it is sent to a human being for review and a decision. Transfers that are "approved" after being rejected are returned for processing with the instruction that the balance check and/or Transaction Limit check be ignored.

Transfers that are "removed" after rejection are either returned to the sender because of insufficient funds or held pending customer instructions. In these cases, customers will usually request a "hold," providing specific information regarding the cover, or request an "exception approval."

When the cause of the rejection is known to the bank—for example, when expected funds have not yet been received—the decision to hold the transfer for later processing is often made by the bank itself.

Although these risk management options are used frequently and are fundamentally necessary in a transfer operation, the volume of transfers is often so heavy that in a high-volume operation these options are used for only a small fraction of the exceptions processed, the "exception handling." In most cases, the transfer is simply returned to the automated process for repeat testing on the assumption that the cover will arrive soon.

Reject-Return Loop, Exception Handling Complications. It is in the reject-return loop that the real complications in exception handling are found. For example:

- How many times and how frequently should the transfer be retested?
- When should the transfer be again rejected and sent for a human decision?
- Should the rejected transfer be queued in First-In, First-Out (FIFO) order for retest?
- Or should it be placed behind more recent transfers to allow for new money?
- Or should the test queue be ordered by amount to allow small transfers through first?
- Or perhaps by amount in reverse order to allow large transfers through first?

Again, given the huge sums involved, these are all important questions with potentially serious financial implications. There are, however, practical limits to the degree of complexity that can be built into a funds-transfer system, and the real challenge therefore is to build a system that implements a reasonable set of trade-offs.

Internal Rules for a Good Wire Transfer System: Example. A good wire transfer system might have the following rules:

- When a transfer is DOL or Limit tested, it is time stamped. Transfers are retested every x minutes. (This would create a potential delay of x minutes or more in the processing of the transfer, but this is better than constant retesting.)
- Transfers are sent for human review only after y minutes of retesting. (This would allow transfers that are now "covered" to be processed (see the preceding rule), but prevent transfers that are still in violation from being repeatedly reviewed by a human being.)
- Transfers are always placed in the queue in FIFO order. (There is a school of thought that says that transfers, once rejected, should be placed at the end of the queue to allow incoming funds an opportunity to accumulate in the account. This makes sense, but it would also allow more recent transfers to be processed before the older items, potentially depleting the funds accumulating in the account and preventing the older transfers from being processed. To avoid this complexity, most banks opt for the FIFO approach—Imagine trying to explain a more complex ordering algorithm to an irate customer.)
- No "automatic" consideration is given to transfer amount. Transfers are always processed in FIFO order. If a decision is made to take a transfer out of the FIFO processing stream, it should be placed in the hold queue and released at a later time. (Is it generally better to pay a large number of small transfers when the account's balance and DOL are smaller than needed, or to pay the transfers in the strict order in which they were received? Again, although there are good arguments for taking transfers out of FIFO order, the complications and potential customer dissatisfaction are not worth the benefit. The compromise here is to allow a human decision maker to take a large-amount transfer out of the contention for account/DOL funds by manually placing it in, and releasing it from, the hold queue.)

Different volume requirements and customer commitments may make this approach inappropriate. However, a well-designed set of rules to handle exceptions is essential.

Other Side of the Transfer

The decision to transfer funds for an individual customer is one side of the coin. On the other side is the decision to pay the money to another bank, settlement system, clearing house, or other payment-system facility. Sometimes the choice is simple and without risk, such as to pay another bank by crediting and debiting accounts at the U.S. Federal Reserve (the "Fed"). Sometimes the decision is more complicated, involving an assessment of money owed by and owed to, such as with the bilateral limits employed by NYCH.

Once in a while, a decision is unnecessary because a system failure, cutoff time violation, communications outage, or other event that was not known when the risk management decision was made on the "source" side of the transfer, stands in the way.

In any case, the result is that only one side of the transfer (the source side) has been executed. This creates an imbalance that also needs to be addressed in the payment system. Should the money earmarked for this transfer be made available for other transfers? Can the transfer be executed made via other means (e.g., transferring via CHIPS rather than the Fed)? Should the transfer be held while the problem is cleared (e.g., by resolving a communication outage)? For how long? Should another intermediary bank be selected? How will that affect the customer?

Although these are valid questions and a good case could be made for many of the actions they imply, few, if any, wire transfer systems (or bank policies) include any risk management response. In effect, most banks separate the two sides of a funds transfer into discrete transactions whereby only the total failure of one of the transactions affects the other side. This approach is again primarily driven by the need to avoid overwhelming complexity in the design, construction, maintenance, and operation of wire transfer systems.

ENDNOTES

1. U.C.C. § 4A-212. The originator's bank, however, may incur an interest obligation under U.C.C. § 4A-210(b). No other exception to the rule in U.C.C. § 4A-212 applies when the bank is the originator's or an intermediary bank. When the receiving bank is the beneficiary's bank, however, the bank may incur an obligation to pay interest if it rejects a payment order after the payment date under U.C.C. § 4A-209(b)(3).
2. Official Comment 1 to U.C.C. § 4A-209.
3. U.C.C. § 4A-210(b).
4. U.C.C. § 4A-301(b). Also see Official Comment 1 to U.C.C. § 4A-301.
5. *Id.* An unexecuted payment order is canceled by operation of law under U.C.C. § 4A-211(d) at the close of the fifth funds-transfer business day of the receiving bank after the execution date or payment date of the order.
6. U.C.C. § 4A-506(b).
7. U.C.C. § 4A-210(a).
8. U.C.C. § 4A-210(b). In the case of a beneficiary's bank, the rejection also prevents acceptance by inaction. See Official Comment 2 to U.C.C. § 4A-210.
9. U.C.C. § 4A-210(a).
10. Official Comment 1 to U.C.C. § 4A-211.
11. U.C.C. § 4A-211(b).
12. U.C.C. § 4A-211(a). Payment orders may be transmitted the same way under U.C.C. § 4A-103(a).
13. U.C.C. § 4A-211(a). The drafting of this provision is not as clear as it might be. First, it could be clearer that the provision refers to security procedures to verify the authenticity of the originator's instructions as opposed to security procedures for the detection of the originator's errors. U.C.C. § 4A-201. Second, the provision seems to suggest that the bank may simply ignore the cancellation or amendment instructions by declining to comply with the security proce-

Endnotes

dure. It seems more likely that the intention of the drafters was to allow the bank to ignore the instructions only after the procedure has been utilized, and, as a result, the instructions appear not to have been authentic.

14. U.C.C. § 4A-211(c).
15. U.C.C. § 4A-106(a) refers to U.C.C. § 1-201(27).
16. Official Comment 3 to U.C.C. § 4A-211.
17. U.C.C. § 4A-211(c). There is an exception, however, to the rule that a payment order may not be canceled or amended after it has been accepted. A payment order issued to the originator's bank may not be accepted by the bank prior to the execution date (or prior to the payment date if the bank is also the originator's bank in a "book transfer" in which the originator and the beneficiary use the same bank). Thus, if the originator's bank executes the order prior to the execution date, the originator may cancel it, leaving the bank with a right to seek recovery from the beneficiary under the law of mistake and restitution. U.C.C. § 4A-209(d).
18. U.C.C. § 4A-211(c). A payment order may also be canceled pursuant to a funds-transfer rule, but such rules generally govern participating banks and not the relationship between the originator and the originator's bank.
19. U.C.C. § 4A-211(c).
20. Official Comment 3 to U.C.C. § 4A-211.
21. *Id.*
22. When the beneficiary's bank has accepted the payment order, cancellation can occur under U.C.C. § 4A-211(c) only under the four specified circumstances. See Chapter 5, page 109.
23. U.C.C. § 4A-211(d). The payment date is the date on which the amount of the order is payable to the beneficiary at the beneficiary's bank. The execution date is the date on which the receiving bank may properly issue its payment order in execution of the payment order it has received. See U.C.C. §§ 4A-401 and 4A-301(b).

24. Official Comment 7 to U.C.C. § 4A-211.
25. U.C.C. § 4A-211(e).
26. U.C.C. § 4A-211(g). The rule is similar to and based on U.C.C. § 4-405(a) with respect to checks.
27. U.C.C. §§ 4A-209(a) and 4A-301(a).
28. U.C.C. § 4A-301(b). See Official Comment 2 to U.C.C. § 4A-301. If the funds transfer is not an ACH transfer, is entirely within the United States, and is to be carried out electronically, the execution date is the payment date specified in the sender's order unless the order is received after the payment date.
29. U.C.C. § 4A-302(a).
30. Official Comment 1 to U.C.C. § 4A-302.
31. U.C.C. § 4A-302(b).
32. Official Comment 2 to U.C.C. § 4A-302.
33. U.C.C. § 4A-302(d).
34. Official Comment 3 to U.C.C. § 4A-302.
35. U.C.C. § 4A-305(a).
36. Official Comment 1 to U.C.C. § 4A-305.
37. In addition to the limited damages available under § 4A-305, if the funds transfer is not completed, the originator and other senders may be entitled to a refund of the amount of the transfer under the "money-back guarantee" provisions discussed in the later section Money-Back Guarantee.
38. "Incidental" expenses are not defined. Presumably, the term refers to minor, foreseeable costs incurred by the originator.
39. U.C.C. § 4A-305(b).
40. U.C.C. § 4A-305(c).
41. The seminal decision is in the nineteenth-century English case *Hadley v. Baxendale*, 9 Ex. 341, 156 Eng. Rep. 145 (1854).
42. Official Comment 2 to U.C.C. § 4A-305.
43. U.C.C. § 4A-305(d). The U.C.C. § 4A-210(b) limit of five funds-transfer business days on the period for which inter-

est is due would seem not to apply when the bank has expressly agreed to pay the order.

44. U.C.C. § 4A-305(e).

45. Official Comment 4 to U.C.C. § 4A-305.

46. For a complete discussion of the negotiation of wire transfer agreements, see Paul S. Turner, *Negotiating Wire Transfer Agreements* (Bethesda, MD: Treasury Management Association (now Association for Financial Professionals), 1996), and Chapter 8 of Paul S. Turner, *Law of Payment Systems and EFT* (New York: Aspen Law and Business, 1999).

47. U.C.C. § 4A-305(f). The provision is preceded by the qualifying phrase "Except as stated in this section," but we are unable to discern any provision of U.C.C. § 4A-305 that permits a receiving bank to vary its liability, except that it may increase its liability under the section by express agreement. See Official Comment 5 to U.C.C. § 4A-305.

48. U.C.C. § 4A-402(c). The originator pays the bank when the originator's bank debits the originator's account to the extent that the debit is covered by a withdrawable credit balance in the account. U.C.C. § 4A-403(a)(3). If the receiving bank is the beneficiary's bank, the payment is due on the payment date under U.C.C. § 4A-402(b).

49. Official Comment 2 to U.C.C. § 4A-402.

50. *Id.*

51. U.C.C. § 4A-402(e).

52. Turner, *Negotiating Wire Transfer Agreements*, 27.

53. U.C.C. § 4A-501(a).

54. U.C.C. §§ 4A-202(b) and 4A-204(a).

55. U.C.C. §§ 4A-202(f) and 4A-204(b).

56. See Chapter 13 in Turner, *Negotiating Wire Transfer Agreements*, and Chapter 8 in Turner, *Law of Payment Systems and EFT.*

57. U.C.C. § 4A-212.

58. U.C.C. § 4A-209(a). See U.C.C. § 4A-301(a) for the definition of execution. Acceptance by the beneficiary's bank is discussed in Chapter 5.

59. U.C.C. § 4A-302(a).

60. U.C.C. § 4A-305.

61. U.C.C. § 4A-402(c).

62. U.C.C. § 4A-402(c) and (d).

63. Some authorities use the term *payment* to refer to the satisfaction of the obligation of the originator to the beneficiary and the term *settlement* to refer to the satisfaction of obligations among banks. See Ernest T. Patrikis, Thomas C. Baxter, Jr., and Raj K. Bhala, *Wire Transfers: A Guide to U.S. and International Laws Governing Funds Transfers* (Rolling Meadows, IL: Bankers Publishing Co., 1993), p. 73: "Payment by the originator to the beneficiary is the purpose of the funds transfer; settlement among banks is essential to effect the funds transfer."

64. U.C.C. § 4A-403(a)(1). Netting under the rules of a funds-transfer system such as CHIPS is covered by U.C.C. § 4A-403(b). Netting between two banks is covered by U.C.C. § 4A-403(c).

65. Official Comment 4 to U.C.C. § 4A-403.

66. U.C.C. § 4A-403(a)(2).

67. U.C.C. § 4A-403(a)(3).

68. In Europe and other parts of the world, industry practice is to wait for cover before making the payment. The SWIFT MT200 series of payments messages, which is widely used in Europe, allows transfer to be matched with cover payments. Although safer, transfer processing is significantly slower, more cumbersome, and prone to error. This is one of the reasons that Europe has only a small portion of the institutional transfer business.

69. A large money center bank on a busy day can reach $50 billion or more of point-in-time payment exposure. Further, if the potential DOL exposure for all customers were added together, it is likely that the potential point-in-time exposure would exceed $1 trillion.

5

Wire Transfers: Completing the Transfer and Rules for Errors

A funds transfer is completed at the last link in the funds-transfer chain when the beneficiary's bank accepts the payment order for the benefit of the beneficiary. Completion of the transfer results in the discharge of the underlying debt of the originator to the beneficiary and the obligation of the beneficiary's bank to pay the beneficiary. This chapter discusses these subjects and concludes with the Rules for Errors for all links in the funds-transfer chain.

LAST LINK IN THE FUNDS-TRANSFER CHAIN

As noted early in Chapter 4, a funds transfer is a series of payment orders, each of which can be viewed as a link in the chain that constitutes the transfer. The last, but not the least important, link in the funds-transfer chain is the payment order to the beneficiary's bank. The order may be sent to the beneficiary's bank by the originator's bank or may be sent by an intermediary bank.

BENEFICIARY AND THE BENEFICIARY'S BANK

Like any other receiving bank, the beneficiary's bank has no obligation to accept a sending bank's payment order.[1]

In other respects, however, the beneficiary's bank is in a very different position than other banks in the funds-transfer chain. The beneficiary's bank is the last bank in the chain, so it cannot "execute" a payment order by sending its own payment order to another bank. Instead, the beneficiary's bank may reject or "accept" the payment order for credit to the account of the beneficiary.

Payment of the Beneficiary and Discharge of the Underlying Obligation between the Originating Company and the Beneficiary

Acceptance by the beneficiary's bank is a very important event because it determines when the beneficiary is entitled to payment by the beneficiary's bank and when the originator's debt to the beneficiary is discharged.

Acceptance by the Beneficiary's Bank. The acceptance of a payment order by the beneficiary is an interbank event because it is another bank's payment order that the beneficiary's bank receives and accepts. That acceptance, however, entitles the beneficiary to be paid.

Acceptance of a Funds-Transfer Order by the Beneficiary: What Can Go Wrong Now? There are four ways in which the beneficiary's bank may accept the order:

1. *Payment to the beneficiary.* The beneficiary's bank may accept the payment order of the sending bank by "paying" the beneficiary.[2] *The mere credit to the beneficiary's account by the beneficiary's bank does not constitute payment.* Payment typically occurs when the bank notifies the ben-

eficiary that the beneficiary may withdraw the amount of the credit.[3] However, payment may also occur when the bank applies the credit to satisfy a debt of the beneficiary or when the funds with the payment order are "otherwise made available" to the beneficiary.[4] An example of the bank otherwise making the funds available is a disbursement of the funds in the form of a "loan" that will be automatically repaid when the beneficiary's bank is paid the amount of the order by the sending bank.[5]

When is the payment final to the beneficiary? When payment has been made to the beneficiary with respect to an obligation incurred by the bank under U.C.C. § 4A-404(a), the payment cannot be recovered by the beneficiary's bank unless subsection (d) or (e) applies.

The exceptions to the finality principle under §4A-405(d) and (e) relate to funds-transfer systems. First, a funds-transfer system rule may provide that a payment to the beneficiary is provisional until receipt of payment by the beneficiary's bank of the payment order it had accepted. If the beneficiary's bank does not receive the payment, the rule is enforceable, provided it requires that the originator and the beneficiary be given notice of the rule and agree to be bound by it.[6]

Second, if the funds-transfer system nets obligations multilaterally and has a loss-sharing agreement among its participants to provide funds when one or more participants do not meet their settlement obligations, the acceptance of the beneficiary's bank may be nullified if the beneficiary's bank accepts a payment order and the system fails to complete settlement under the system's rules. Under these circumstances, the beneficiary's bank is entitled to recover its payment to the beneficiary.[7]

In the absence of these two exceptions, payment is final under § 4A-405.

2. *Notification of the beneficiary.* Acceptance of the payment order also occurs when the bank notifies the beneficiary

that it has received the order or that the account has been credited in the amount of the order, unless the notice states that the bank is rejecting the order or that the funds may not be withdrawn or used until the bank receives payment for the order by the sender.[8] The Official Comments explain how notice can constitute acceptance:

> The beneficiary's bank may also accept by notifying the beneficiary that the order has been received. "Notifies" is defined in Section 1-201(26).[9] In some cases a beneficiary's bank will receive a payment order during the day but settlement of the sender's obligation to pay the order will not occur until the end of the day. If the beneficiary's bank wants to defer incurring liability to the beneficiary until the beneficiary's bank receives payment, it can do so. The beneficiary's bank incurs no liability with respect to a payment order that it receives until it accepts the order.[10]

However, the bank may accept the order before the beneficiary's bank has been paid by the sender by giving notice to the beneficiary of the receipt of the order or by making a withdrawable credit of the amount of the order to the beneficiary's account.

3. *Passive acceptance by payment by the sending bank.* The beneficiary's bank may accept the payment order by waiting until the bank receives the sender's payment for the order.[11] Payment and settlement among the bank participants in a funds transfer is discussed in Chapter 4. The Official Comments explain:

> If the sender is a bank and the beneficiary's bank receives payment from the sender through the Federal Reserve System or a funds transfer system (Section 4A-403(a)(1)) or, less commonly, through credit to an account of the beneficiary's bank with

the sender or another bank (Section 4A-403(a)(2)), acceptance by the beneficiary's bank occurs at the time payment is made. . . . Section 4A-209(b)(2) results in automatic acceptance of payment orders issued to a beneficiary's bank by means of Fedwire because the Federal Reserve account of the beneficiary's bank is credited and final payment is made to that bank when the payment order is received.[12]

Acceptance can occur as a result of the sender's payment of its obligation to pay if the beneficiary's bank pays the wrong person by mistake. The result would be unfortunate for the bank. For example, assume that the beneficiary's bank is supposed to pay John Doe but instead pays Richard Roe. No acceptance occurs when the bank pays Richard Roe, of course, because John Doe has not been paid or notified that the funds are available. However, when the sender pays the beneficiary's bank, passive acceptance occurs by the receipt of the payment. Because the bank has accepted the order, it is liable to pay John Doe. The bank may seek recovery of the funds from Richard Roe under the law governing mistake and restitution.[13]

4. *Passive acceptance by ability to debit sender.* If the sender has an account with the beneficiary's bank, the beneficiary's bank can debit the sender's account to satisfy the sender's obligation to pay its order to the beneficiary's account, provided that the amount of the sender's order is fully covered. However, transfers may be coming into and going out of the account during the day, and some transfers into the account may not occur until late in the day or after the close of the banking day. As a result, the beneficiary's bank may not be able to determine until the end of the day on the payment date (the date on which the beneficiary is to be paid[14]) whether the amount of the sender's order is fully covered.

Under these circumstances, acceptance can occur on the opening of the next funds-transfer business day

107

following the payment date if, at that time, the amount of the payment order is fully covered by a withdrawable credit balance in an authorized account of the sender (or if the beneficiary's bank has otherwise been fully paid by the sender). However, the beneficiary's bank may prevent such acceptance by a timely rejection of the payment order. The beneficiary's bank may reject the order:

- Before the opening of the funds-transfer business day of the bank following the payment date,
- Within one hour after the opening of the day described in the first deadline, or
- Within one hour after the opening of the next business day *of the sender* following the payment date if that time is later than the time in the second deadline.

The last deadline permits a bank to give notice of rejection of a payment order when the sender is in an earlier time zone. The notice is given within one hour of the opening of business of the sender. The Official Comments give an example of how the deadline works:

> For example, the sender may be located in California and the beneficiary's bank in New York. Since in most cases notice of rejection would be communicated electronically or by telephone, it might not be feasible for the bank to give notice before one hour after the opening of the funds transfer business day in New York because at that hour, the sender's business day may not have started in California. For that reason, there are alternative deadlines stated in [§ 4A-209(b)(3)]. In the case stated, the bank acts in time if it gives notice within one hour after the opening of the business day of the sender.[15]

However, when the notice of rejection is received by the sender after the payment date and the sender's account does not bear interest, the beneficiary's bank incurs an interest obligation to the sender.[16]

> In that case the bank had the use of funds of the sender that the sender could reasonably assume would be used to pay the beneficiary. The rate of interest is stated in Section 4A-506. If the sender receives notice on the day after the payment date, the sender is entitled to one day's interest. If receipt of notice is delayed for more than one day, the sender is entitled to interest for each additional day of delay.[17]

Cancellation and Amendment of Payment Orders. The cancellation and amendment of payment orders issued to banks that are not the beneficiary's bank are discussed in Chapter 4. After a payment order has been accepted by a bank, the general rule is that the order can be canceled or amended only with the agreement of the bank. That rule applies to orders accepted by the beneficiary's bank as well.

Article 4A is more restrictive, however, with respect to payment orders issued to the beneficiary's bank. Acceptance determines when the originator's obligation to the beneficiary is discharged, and the drafters of Article 4A thought that it would be inappropriate to allow the beneficiary's bank to agree to a cancellation or amendment except in unusual cases.[18] Thus, even with the agreement of the bank, after the order is accepted, cancellation or amendment of the order may occur only if the order was issued:

  (i) in execution of an unauthorized payment order or

 (ii) because of a mistake by a sender in the funds transfer which resulted in the issuance of an order that

    (a) is a duplicate of an order previously issued,

    (b) orders payment to a beneficiary not entitled to payment, or

    (c) orders payment in an amount greater than the amount that the beneficiary is entitled to receive.[19]

The Official Comments illustrate postacceptance cancellation or amendment of payment orders issued to the beneficiary's bank:

Case 1. Originator's Bank executed a payment order issued in the name of its customer as sender. The order was not authorized by the customer and was fraudulently issued. Beneficiary's Bank accepted the payment order issued by Originator's Bank. Under [§ 4A-211(c)(2)] Originator's Bank can cancel the order if Beneficiary's Bank consents. It doesn't make any difference whether the payment order that Originator's Bank accepted was or was not enforceable against the customer under Section 4A-202(b). Verification under that provision is important in determining whether Originator's Bank or the customer has the risk of loss, but it has no relevance under Section 4A-211(c)(2). Whether or not verified, the payment order was not authorized by the customer. Cancellation of the payment order to Beneficiary's Bank causes the acceptance of Beneficiary's Bank to be nullified. [§ 4A-211(e).] Beneficiary's Bank is entitled to recover payment from the beneficiary to the extent allowed by the law of mistake and restitution. In this kind of case the beneficiary is usually a party to the fraud who has no right to receive or retain payment of the order.

Case 2. Originator owed Beneficiary $1,000,000 and ordered Bank A to pay that amount to the account of Beneficiary in Bank B. Bank A issued a complying order to Bank B, but by mistake issued a duplicate order as well. Bank B accepted both orders. Under [§ 4A-211(c)(2)] cancellation of the duplicate order could be made by Bank A with the consent of Bank B. Beneficiary has no right to receive or retain payment of the duplicate payment order if only $1,000,000 was owed by Originator to Beneficiary.

Case 3. Originator owed $1,000,000 to X. Intending to pay X, Originator ordered Bank A to pay $1,000,000 to Y's account in Bank B. Bank A issued a complying payment order to Bank B which Bank B accepted by releasing the $1,000,000 to Y. Under [§ 4A-211(c)(ii)] Bank A can cancel its order to Bank B with the consent of Bank B if Y was not entitled to receive payment from the Originator. Originator can also cancel its order to Bank A with Bank A's consent. [§ 4A-211(c)(1).]

Case 4. Originator owed Beneficiary $10,000. By mistake Originator ordered Bank A to pay $1,000,000 to the account of Beneficiary in Bank B. Bank A issued a complying order to Bank B which accepted by notifying Beneficiary of its right to withdraw $1,000,000. Cancellation is permitted in this case under [§ 4A-211(c)(2)(iii)]. If Bank B paid Beneficiary, it is entitled to recover the payment except to the extent the law of mistake and restitution allows Beneficiary to retain $10,000, the amount of the debt owed to Beneficiary.[20]

Obligation of the Bank to Pay the Beneficiary. When the beneficiary's bank accepts a payment order, the bank becomes obligated to pay the beneficiary the amount of the order.[21] Payment is due on the payment date of the order, the day when the order is payable to the beneficiary,[22] unless the acceptance is after the close of the funds-transfer business day, in which case payment is due on the next funds-transfer business day.[23]

The obligation of the beneficiary's bank to pay the beneficiary after accepting the payment order was thought by the Article 4A drafters to be a very serious obligation. Thus, if the bank fails to pay and is notified of the particular circumstances that might give rise to the beneficiary's sustaining consequential damages, the beneficiary can recover the consequential damages unless the bank can prove that it had a reasonable doubt concerning the right of the beneficiary to payment.[24] Moreover, the obligation of the beneficiary's bank to pay the beneficiary cannot be disclaimed by the bank in an agreement between the bank and the beneficiary.[25]

The Official Comments discuss the beneficiary's right to recover consequential damages:

> [Section 4A-404(a)] provides that the beneficiary of an accepted payment order may recover consequential damages if the beneficiary's bank refuses to pay the order after demand by the beneficiary if the bank at that time had notice of the particular circumstances giving rise to the damages. Such damages are recoverable only to the extent that the bank had "notice of the damages." The quoted phrase requires that the bank have notice of the general type or nature of the damages that will be suffered as a result of the refusal to pay and their general magnitude. There is no requirement that the bank have notice of the exact or even the approximate amount of the damages, but if the amount of damages is extraordinary the bank is entitled to notice of that fact. For example, in *Evra Corp. v. Swiss Bank Corp.*,[26] failure to complete a funds transfer of only $27,000 required to retain rights to a very favorable ship charter resulted in a claim for more than $2,000,000 of consequential damages. Since it is not reasonably foreseeable that a failure to make a relatively small payment will result in damages of this magnitude, notice is not sufficient if the beneficiary's bank has notice only that the $27,000 is necessary to retain rights on a ship charter. The bank is entitled to notice that an exceptional amount of damages will result as well. For example, there would be adequate notice if the bank had been made aware that damages of $1,000,000 or more might result.[27]

Consequential damages are not available when the refusal of the beneficiary's bank to pay the beneficiary is based on "a reasonable doubt concerning the right of the beneficiary to payment." The Official Comments explain that the "reasonable doubt" exception to the obligation of the beneficiary's bank to pay the beneficiary does not apply to a dispute between the originator and the beneficiary:

> For example, the originator may try to prevent payment to the beneficiary by the beneficiary's bank by alleging that the beneficiary is not entitled to payment because of fraud against the originator or a breach of contract relating to the obligation. The fraud or breach of contract claim of the originator may be grounds for recovery by the originator from the beneficiary after the beneficiary is paid, but it does not affect the obligation of the beneficiary's bank to pay the beneficiary. Unless the payment order has been cancelled pursuant to Section 4A-211(c), there is no excuse for refusing to pay the beneficiary and, in a proper case, the refusal may result in consequential damages. Except in the case of a book transfer, in which the beneficiary's bank is also the originator's bank, the originator of a funds transfer cannot cancel a payment order to the beneficiary's bank, with or without the consent of the beneficiary's bank, because the originator is not the sender of that order. Thus, the beneficiary's bank may safely ignore any instruction by the originator to withhold payment to the beneficiary.[28]

If the payment order instructs payment to a particular account of the beneficiary, the bank must notify the beneficiary of its receipt of the order before midnight of the next funds-transfer business day following the payment date. If the order does not instruct payment to an account of the beneficiary, the notice is required only if the payment order requires it. If the bank fails to give the required notice, the bank must pay interest from the day notice should have been given until the day the beneficiary learns of the bank's receipt of the payment order. No other damages arc recoverable, but if the beneficiary must sue to compel the bank to pay the interest, the beneficiary may recover its reasonable attorney's fees.[29]

The Official Comments observe that if acceptance occurs under the provisions that involve the beneficiary's bank giving notice of receipt of the order to the beneficiary, as it often does, the notice would be given in any event. The obligation to give notice thus will be meaningful only when acceptance occurs under other provisions, such as when the acceptance occurs because the beneficiary's bank receives payment for the payment order.[30]

Payment to Beneficiary and Discharge of Debt of Originator. Funds transfers normally serve the purpose of discharging an obligation, such as to pay for goods or services, to pay the purchase price in an acquisition, or to repay an indebtedness. It was noted earlier that when the beneficiary's bank accepts a payment order, the beneficiary becomes obligated to pay the beneficiary's bank. The payment is not due until the payment date, but the obligation is incurred upon the bank's acceptance of the payment order.[31] At the same time, the obligation of the originator to the beneficiary is discharged.[32] Thus, the obligation of the originator to pay the beneficiary is replaced by the obligation of the beneficiary's bank.

Section 4A-406(a) states the "fundamental rule"[33] that the originator's payment to the beneficiary in a funds transfer occurs when the beneficiary's bank accepts the payment order for the beneficiary. Section 4A-406(b) states that if the payment was made to satisfy an obligation of the originator, the obligation is discharged "to the same extent discharge would result from payment to the beneficiary of the same amount in money."

Discharge does not occur, however, when:

- The payment was by a means prohibited by a contract with the beneficiary,
- The beneficiary within a reasonable time after receiving notice of the receipt of the payment order by the bank

notified the originator that the beneficiary refused the payment,

- The funds received by the beneficiary's bank were not withdrawn by the beneficiary or applied to a debt of the beneficiary, and
- The beneficiary would suffer a loss that could reasonably have been avoided if the payment had been by a means that complied with the contract.

The mere fact that the originator breached a contract obligation by paying via a funds transfer rather than by other means does not mean that the beneficiary has sustained any loss. The law discharges the debt of the originator despite the breach unless the breach has caused a loss to the beneficiary and all of the other conditions specified above are satisfied.

When the originator's breach has caused a loss to the beneficiary, the purpose of the exception to the rule that the bank's acceptance discharges the originator's obligation is to allocate the risk of the insolvency of the beneficiary's bank. The Official Comments explain the discharge rules:

In a large percentage of funds transfers, the transfer is made to pay an obligation of the originator. [Section 4A-406(a)] states that the beneficiary is paid by the originator when the beneficiary's bank accepts a payment order for the benefit of the beneficiary. When that happens, the effect under [§ 4A-406(b)] is to substitute the obligation of the beneficiary's bank for the obligation of the originator. The effect is similar to that under Article 3 if a cashier's check payable to the beneficiary had been taken by the beneficiary. Normally, payment by funds transfer is sought by the beneficiary because it puts money into the hands of the beneficiary more quickly. As a practical matter the beneficiary and the originator nearly always agree to the funds transfer in advance. Under [§ 4A-406(b)] acceptance by the beneficiary's bank will result in discharge of the obligation for which payment was made unless the beneficiary has made a contract with respect to the obligation which did not permit payment by the means used. Thus, if there is no contract of the beneficiary with respect to the means of payment of the obligation, acceptance by the beneficiary's bank of a payment order to the account of the beneficiary can result in discharge.[34]

The Official Comments give examples of the exception to the rule that acceptance by the beneficiary's bank results in the discharge of the originator's obligation to the beneficiary:

Suppose Beneficiary's contract stated that payment of an obligation owed by Originator was to be made by a cashier's check of Bank A. Instead, Originator paid by a funds transfer to Beneficiary's account in Bank B. Bank B accepted a payment order for the benefit of Beneficiary by immediately notifying Beneficiary that the funds were available for withdrawal. Before Beneficiary had a reasonable opportunity to withdraw the funds, Bank B suspended payments [i.e., filed for relief in insolvency proceedings]. Under the unless clause of [§ 4A-406(b)] Beneficiary is not required to accept the payment as discharging the obligation owed by Originator to Beneficiary if Beneficiary's contract means that Beneficiary was not required to accept payment by wire transfer. Beneficiary could refuse the funds transfer as payment of the obligation and could resort to rights under the underlying contract to enforce the obligation. The rationale is that Originator cannot impose the risk of Bank B's insolvency on Beneficiary if Beneficiary had specified another means of payment that did not entail that risk. If Beneficiary is required to accept Originator's payment, Beneficiary would suffer a loss that would not have occurred if payment had been made by a cashier's check on Bank A, and Bank A had not suspended payments. In this case Originator will have to pay twice. It is obliged to pay the amount of its payment order to the bank that accepted it and has to pay the obligation it owes to the Beneficiary which has not been discharged.[35]

The Originator would have the right, however, to seek recovery from Bank B.[36] The Official Comments give another example of the application of the exception to the discharge rule in which the exception does not apply and the obligation is thereby discharged:

> Suppose Beneficiary's contract called for payment by a Fedwire transfer to Bank B, but the payment order accepted by Bank B was not a Fedwire transfer. Before the funds were withdrawn by Beneficiary, Bank B suspended payments. The sender of the payment order to Bank B paid the amount of the order to Bank B. In this case the payment by Originator did not comply with Beneficiary's contract, but the noncompliance did not result in a loss to Beneficiary as required by [§ 4A-406(b)(iv)]. A Fedwire transfer avoids the risk of the insolvency of the sender of the payment order to Bank B, but it does not affect the risk that Bank B will suspend payments before withdrawal of the funds by Beneficiary. Thus, the unless clause of [§ 4A-406(b)] is not applicable and the obligation owed to Beneficiary is discharged.

As noted earlier, the discharge would occur despite the deduction by a bank of its charges in the funds-transfer transaction. If an intermediary bank charges $10 in the transaction, for example, and the beneficiary receives $999,990 in satisfaction of indebtedness of $1,000,000, the debt is nevertheless discharged unless the beneficiary demands payment of, and the originator fails to pay, the $10 charge.[37]

Interest Compensation. A receiving bank is required to pay interest to the sender when:

- The bank is liable to the customer for a fraudulent transfer that was duly reported by the customer,[38]
- The sender receives notice of the rejection of a payment order by the beneficiary's bank after the payment date of the order,[39]
- The bank fails to execute a payment order without giving a notice of rejection and the sender's account has sufficient funds to cover the order,[40]
- Improper execution by the bank results in the delay of payment to the beneficiary,[41]
- The receiving bank is obliged to refund the sender's payment under the "money-back guarantee,"[42] or
- The beneficiary's bank fails to give the required notice to the beneficiary of the bank's receipt of the payment order.[43]

The receiving bank and the sender in the funds-transfer transaction may agree on the terms of interest payable by the bank to the sender. Such terms may also be established by a funds-transfer system rule. In the absence of an agreement or funds-transfer system rule, the terms of the interest compensation payable by a receiving bank to a sender are governed by § 4A-506.[44]

The rate of interest is the average of the Federal Funds Rates published by the Federal Reserve Bank of New York for each of the days for which interest is payable divided by 360 (360 days basis). The amount of interest is determined by multiplying the rate by the amount on which interest is payable and multiplying the product by the number of days for which interest is payable. If on any of those days a published rate is not available, the rate for that day is the same as the published rate for the next preceding day for which a rate is available.[45] If the interest is payable because the transfer was not completed but the failure to complete the transfer was not due to the fault of the bank, the interest is reduced by the percentage equal to the reserve requirement on deposits of the bank.[46]

The Official Comments provide the following example:

> A bank is obliged to pay interest on $1,000,000 for three days, July 3, July 4, and July 5. The published Fed Funds rate is .082 for July 3 and .081 for July 5. There is no published rate for July 4 because that is not a banking day. The rate for July 3 applies to July 4. The applicable Federal Funds rate is .08167 (the average of .082, .082, and .081) divided by 360 which equals .0002268. The amount of interest payable is $1,000,000 × .0002268 × 3 = $680.40.[47]

Set-Off, Priority, and Litigation. Suppose that the beneficiary owes its bank $1,000 and the bank receives a $1,000 payment order for the beneficiary. May the bank apply the funds to set off the debt of its beneficiary? Yes; § 4A-502(c) states that after the bank credits the beneficiary's account, the amount credited "may be set off against an obligation owed by the beneficiary by the bank."

Suppose that the customer's bank receives a payment order from the customer at 10:00 A.M. to pay Company X $1,000, an order from the customer at 10:05 A.M. to pay Company Y $1,500, and another from the customer at 10:30 A.M. to pay Company Z $2,000. At 10:35 the bank decides to act on the three orders, but there is only $2,000 in the account. May the bank execute the order for $2,000 even though it was the last order it received? Yes; the bank may execute the customer's orders in any sequence.[48]

Suppose that a bank finds itself in litigation with another party to the funds transfer. What law applies in the litigation? The parties may by agreement choose the applicable law.[49] If they do not do so:

- The rights and obligations between a sender and a receiving bank are governed by the law of the jurisdiction in which the receiving bank is located,

- The rights and obligations between the beneficiary's bank and the beneficiary are governed by the law of the jurisdiction in which the beneficiary's bank is located, and
- The issue of when payment is made by the originator to the beneficiary is governed by the law of the jurisdiction in which the beneficiary's bank is located.[50]

Suppose that the customer is squabbling with its creditors. The bank receives a payment order instructing the bank to pay Creditor X. The bank executes the order in reliance on there being sufficient withdrawable funds in the customer's account to cover the order. Before the bank debits the customer's account, however, the bank is served with creditor process by Creditor Y attaching the funds in the account. If the attachment is valid and the bank must pay Creditor Y, there will be insufficient funds to cover the payment order issued to pay Creditor X. Under these circumstances the bank is allowed to debit the customer's account to pay for the order it issued despite the process served by Creditor Y.[51]

MANAGING RISKS IN THE LINKS OF THE WIRE TRANSFER PAYMENT SYSTEM

Beneficiary and the Beneficiary's Bank

The beneficiary and the originator both expect that the beneficiary will receive the amount of a wire transfer from the beneficiary's bank.

This section discusses the legal solutions to the complicated situations than can arise when the funds have been transferred but the beneficiary has not received the funds. Once the bank has accepted the final payment order, the last link in the funds-transfer chain, the beneficiary is entitled to payment. If the bank has credited the funds to the wrong account, the beneficiary is entitled to be paid by the bank. If the bank has exercised any set-off rights against the transferred funds, then the beneficiary will be deemed to have been paid to the extent that the bank has set off an amount equivalent to the bank's claim against the beneficiary.

The originator may arrange with the beneficiary that the beneficiary will confirm receipt of wire transfer payments. Doing so will help to ensure that the originator will know when the transferred funds have actually been received by the beneficiary, and if they have not been received, the originator will know that as well. That type of arrangement is especially appropriate when funds are transferred in very large amounts, or are wired as part of contractual closing requirements, and in other situations in which the parties agree that confirmation is appropriate. Such arrangements do not directly involve the sending, intermediary, or receiving banks.

RULES FOR ERRORS

The general rule with respect to errors under Article 4A is that the customer and the bank are each liable for their own errors. The general rule is not explicitly stated as such in Article 4A, but it may be extrapolated from all of the rules relating to the errors of the parties in the funds-transfer chain.[52]

Errors can occur at each link in the chain. The customer may commit an error in the first payment order in the chain that originates the funds transfer. The customer's bank may commit an error in the payment order it issues in execution of the order. An intermediary bank may commit an error when it executes the payment order it receives, and the beneficiary's bank may commit an error when it accepts the final payment order in the funds-transfer chain.

This section examines the rules applicable to the errors that may be committed in the course of a funds transfer by the various parties to the transfer, beginning with the customer's errors.

General Rule for Customer Errors

The general rule is that the Customer is liable for its own errors contained in any payment order issued to the customer's bank.

The general rule is not explicitly stated in Article 4A but is implicit in § 4A-302(a)(1).

A receiving bank has no obligation to execute a payment order it has received.[53] If the bank nevertheless accepts the order, however, § 4A-302(a) states that the bank is obliged to issue "a payment order complying with the sender's order" and also obliged to follow the sender's instructions concerning:

- Any intermediary bank or funds-transfer system to be used in carrying out the funds transfer, or
- The means by which payment orders are to be transmitted in the funds transfer.

Moreover, the originator's bank is obliged to instruct the intermediary bank according to the instruction of the originator.

Stated otherwise, if the payment order of the customer contains an error, the bank is obliged to perpetuate the error because the bank is obliged to comply with the customer's instructions. On this basis, the bank cannot be held liable for the customer's errors.

Special rules apply, however, to errors designated by Article 4A as "misdescription" errors and when the bank and the customer have agreed that the bank will use a security procedure to detect the customer's errors. These rules are discussed in the following paragraphs.

Misdescription Errors

Probably the most common form of customer error is a **misdescription** error. A misdescription occurs when the customer identifies the beneficiary or a bank in the funds-transfer transaction by both a name and a number, and the name and number identify different persons, that is, either the name or the number is erroneous. Liability for losses resulting from the misdescription of the beneficiary is covered by § 4A-207, and liability for losses resulting from the misdescription of a bank is covered by § 4A-208.

Misdescription of the Beneficiary. In a typical case involving the misdescription of the beneficiary, the customer's payment order to its bank identifies the beneficiary by a name and a number. The name and number refer to different persons. The name is correct, but the number identifies the wrong person. When the payment order reaches the beneficiary's bank, the bank ignores the name and processes the payment order on the basis of the number. As a result, the funds are credited to the wrong person. If the funds cannot be recovered from that person, who is liable for the loss: the customer or the beneficiary's bank?

General Rule for Beneficiary Misdescription. The general rule for beneficiary misdescription imposes liability on the customer. The beneficiary's bank is allowed to rely on the number and ignore the name. Section 4A-207 provides that if a payment order received by the beneficiary's bank "identifies the beneficiary both by name and by an identifying or bank account number and the name and number identify different persons," the beneficiary's bank "may rely on the number as the proper identification of the beneficiary of the order."[54] Moreover, the bank has no duty to determine whether the name and number refer to the same person.[55]

The reason for the rule is that banks normally process payment orders by automated means that identify the beneficiary by number and are not capable of identifying the beneficiary by name. The Article 4A drafters, consistent with their goal of maintaining the high-speed, low-cost features of funds transfers, wanted to facilitate the continued use of automated means. The Official Comments explain the rule:

> A very large percentage of payment orders issued to the beneficiary's bank by another bank are processed by automated means using machines capable of reading orders on standard formats that identify the beneficiary by an identifying number or the number of a bank account. The processing of the order by the beneficiary's bank and

the crediting of the beneficiary's account are done by use of the identifying or bank account number without human reading of the payment order itself. The process is comparable to that used in automated payment of checks. The standard format, however, may also allow the inclusion of the name of the beneficiary and other information which can be useful to the beneficiary's bank and the beneficiary but which plays no part in the process of payment. If the beneficiary's bank has both the account number and name of the beneficiary supplied by the originator of the funds transfer, it is possible for the beneficiary's bank to determine whether the name and number refer to the same person, but if a duty to make that determination is imposed on the beneficiary's bank the benefits of automated payment are lost. Manual handling of payment orders is both expensive and subject to human error. If payment orders can be handled on an automated basis there are substantial economies of operation and the possibility of clerical error is reduced.[56]

Exceptions to the General Rule.   There are two exceptions to the general rule:

1. The customer's bank is liable for the loss when it has not notified the originating customer that the beneficiary's bank might pay on the basis of the number (unless the originator is also a bank), and
2. The beneficiary's bank is liable for the loss when the bank knows that the name and number refer to different persons.

Customer's Bank Liable for Failure to Give Notice.   Liability for a loss resulting from a customer's misdescription error shifts from the customer to the customer's bank when the customer's bank has failed to give the customer notice that the beneficiary's bank may rely on the number. To avoid the loss, the bank must prove that the customer:

had notice that payment of a payment order issued by the originator might be made by the beneficiary's bank on the basis of an identifying or bank account number even if it identifies a person different from the named beneficiary.[57]

The notice need not be given, however, when the originator is also a bank. The purpose of the rule shifting liability to the customer's bank is to protect customers who may not be aware that the beneficiary's bank might process the payment order on the basis of the number. Banks, however, are thought not to need such protection.

> [Section 4A-207(c)] is designed to protect the originator . . . . Under that [section], the originator is responsible for the inconsistent description of the beneficiary if it had notice that the order might be paid by the beneficiary's bank on the basis of the number. If the originator is a bank, the originator always has that responsibility. The rationale is that any bank should know how payment orders are processed and paid. If the originator is not a bank, the originator's bank must prove that its customer, the originator, had notice.[58]

The notice may be included in a Funds Transfer Services Agreement or provided to the customer in a separate document or even, it appears, provided orally:

> Notice can be proved by any admissible evidence, but the bank can always provide notice by providing the customer with a written statement of the required information and obtaining the customer's signature to the statement. The statement will then apply to any payment order accepted by the bank thereafter. The information need not be supplied more than once.[59]

The most effective way to prove that the notice has been given is to produce the notice signed by the customer, and the most efficient way to obtain the customer's signature on the notice is to insert it into the Funds Transfer Services Agreement. Good banking practice thus dictates that every customer sign an Agreement and every Agreement contain the notice. The notice should state that the beneficiary's bank might make payment on the basis of the number "even if it identifies a person different from the named beneficiary."[60]

Beneficiary's Bank Liable When Aware of Discrepancy. Under the general rule, the beneficiary's bank, in processing a payment order in which the beneficiary is misdescribed, may rely on the number and ignore the name. If the bank processes the payment order on the basis of the name and a loss results from the misdescription, the beneficiary's bank is liable for the loss.[61]

Moreover, the general rule applies only when the "beneficiary's bank does not know that the name and number refer to different persons."[62] Thus, the beneficiary's bank is liable for losses when it has "knowledge" that the name and number refer to different persons.

How might such knowledge be acquired by the beneficiary's bank? Under the general rules and definitions of the Uniform Commercial Code, a party in a transaction is regarded as having "knowledge" of a fact when it is brought to the attention of the individual conducting the transaction or when the fact would have been brought to the attention of that individual if the party had exercised "due diligence."[63]

On this basis, the beneficiary's bank would have "knowledge" that the name and number refer to different persons when that fact is brought to the attention of the individual conducting the transaction in the bank's wire room or when that fact should have been brought to the attention of that individual if the beneficiary's bank had exercised due diligence. In normal circumstances the bank can be expected to exercise due diligence, and thus the "knowledge" exception to the general rule that the beneficiary's bank may rely on the number and ignore the name, would normally present no problem to the bank. The bank would typically not have knowledge of the name and number discrepancy, and when it had actual knowledge it would not accept the payment order.

The capability of modern computers, however, poses uncertainty in the rules. Suppose that the bank's software is capable of alerting the wire room personnel to the existence of a name in the payment order. Does due diligence require the wire room personnel to check the name against the account number to be certain that the name and number match? Perhaps not. Article 4A makes clear that the beneficiary's bank "need not determine whether the name and number refer to the same person."[64]

Fraudulently Induced Misdescription. The foregoing rules may apply to relieve the beneficiary's bank of liability when it has relied on the number in processing a misdescribed payment if the misdescription has been fraudulently induced. The Official Comments give an example of a thief fraudulently inducing an originator to issue a payment order in which the name and number refer to different persons:

> Doe is the holder of shares in Mutual Fund. Thief, impersonating Doe, requests redemption of the shares and directs Mutual Fund to wire the redemption proceeds to Doe's account #12345 in Beneficiary's Bank. Mutual Funds originates a funds transfer by issuing a payment order to Originator's Bank to make a payment to Doe's account #12345 in Beneficiary's Bank. Originator's Bank executes the order by issuing a conforming order to Beneficiary's Bank, which makes payment to account #12345. That account is the account of Roe rather than Doe.[65]

In the foregoing example, Thief has fraudulently induced Mutual Fund to issue a payment order in which the beneficiary is misdescribed. The name of the beneficiary, Doe, is correct, but the number of the account, #12345, refers to the account of Roe, not Doe. The rules described above would apply. Beneficiary's Bank would be entitled to rely on the number, and Mutual Fund would be required to reimburse Originator's Bank for the funds transfer, unless one of the exceptions described earlier applies.

In the example, Roe may be Thief, a confederate of Thief, or an innocent third party. The Official Comments illustrate how Roe might be an innocent third party:

> Assume that Roe is a gem merchant that agreed to sell gems to Thief who agreed to wire the purchase price to Roe's account at Beneficiary's Bank. Roe believed that a credit to Roe's account was a transfer of funds from Thief and released the gems to Thief in good faith in reliance on the payment.[66]

Whether Roe is the thief, a confederate, or an innocent third party, the beneficiary's bank would be entitled to rely on the number under the general rule. Thus, Mutual Fund would be obligated to pay its bank unless the exceptions to the general rule applied, that is, unless the bank had failed to give notice to Mutual Fund that the beneficiary's bank might rely on the number (in which case Mutual Fund's bank is liable for the loss) or the beneficiary's bank accepted the order with knowledge that the name and number were discrepant (in which case the beneficiary's bank is liable for the loss). Mutual Fund would be entitled to pursue the wrongdoer under the law of mistake and restitution if the wrongdoer can be found.[67]

Misdescription of a Bank

In addition to misdescribing the beneficiary, a customer may misdescribe the beneficiary's bank or misdescribe an intermediary bank. The Official Comments provide an example of the misdescription of an intermediary bank:

Suppose Originator issues a payment order to Originator's Bank that instructs the bank to use an intermediary bank identified as Bank A and by an identifying number #67890. The identifying number refers to Bank B. Originator intended to identify Bank A as intermediary bank.[68]

In this example, the funds-transfer instructions would be received by Bank B instead of by Bank A. As a result, the funds transfer may not be completed or it may be delayed. Under § 4A-302(a)(1)(i), a receiving bank is obliged to comply with the sender's instructions concerning any intermediary bank to be used in carrying out a funds transfer. Liability for failure to comply with the instructions is limited to interest, the originator's funds-transfer expenses, and incidental expenses.[69] Whether the Originator's Bank is liable for a breach of that obligation in the example depends on whether the Originator's Bank has given notice to the Originator that it might rely on the number. If it has given the notice, it avoids the liability.[70]

Thus, liability under § 4A-208 with respect to a misdescribed bank is very much like liability under § 4A-208 with respect to a misdescribed beneficiary. If the Originator's Bank can prove that the Originator had notice that the bank might rely on the number as the proper identification of an intermediary bank or a beneficiary's bank, the bank is not liable to the Originator under § 4A-302. If the bank cannot prove that the Originator had the notice, the bank must pay the Originator interest losses and the Originator's expenses. The notice should state that the bank might make payment on the basis of the number "even if it identifies a person different from the bank identified by name."[71] For an example of a notice under § 4A-207, see § 2.3.2 of the American Bar Association's Model Funds Transfer Services Agreement.[72]

The rules for misdescribed banks are different in a few respects, however, from those for misdescribed beneficiaries.

First, the receiving bank may rely on the name as well as the number unless it knows that the name and number identify different persons. The bank need not determine whether the name and number identify different persons.[73] The Official Comments do not explain, and it is not clear, why the bank may rely on the name or number in the case of misdescribed banks but not in the case of misdescribed beneficiaries.

Second, it is clear that in the case of a misdescribed beneficiary, the customer need not reimburse the bank (and if the customer has paid the bank, the customer is entitled to a refund) when payment has been wrongful. Payment would be wrongful when the wrong person has been paid and the bank has relied on the name or knew that the name and number identified different persons.[74] An analogous rule with respect to misdescribed banks would require the bank to reimburse the customer when the bank has executed the customer's order with knowledge that the name and number identify different persons. The analogous rule is omitted.[75]

The third difference relates to the bank's expenses. If the customer has misdescribed an intermediary bank or the beneficiary's bank, and the receiving bank has executed the customer's order based on the number, the customer must compensate the bank for the bank's losses or expenses resulting from the bank's reliance on the number.[76]

Error-Detection Security Procedures

Article 4A distinguishes between errors that result in the erroneous transfer of funds and less significant errors that result in a party's incurring incidental expenses, delay, or loss of interest. Under § 4A-205, the customer may avoid loss when funds are transferred from the customer's account as a result of the customer's errors when the bank has failed to comply with a **security procedure** for the detection of errors.

The Official Comment describes the types of loss covered by § 4A-205:

This section concerns errors in the content or in the transmission of payment orders. It deals with three kinds of errors. *Case 1.* The order identifies a beneficiary not intended by the sender. For example, Sender intends to wire funds to a beneficiary identified only by account number. The wrong account number is stated in the order. *Case 2.* The error is in the amount of the order. For example, Sender intends to wire $1,000 to Beneficiary. Through error, the payment order instructs payment of $1,000,000. *Case 3.* A payment order is sent to the receiving bank and then, by mistake, the same payment order is sent to the receiving bank again.[77]

In these examples, the bank complies with the customer's erroneous instructions, the funds are transferred from the customer's account, and the customer sustains the loss:

In Case 3, the receiving bank may have no way of knowing whether the second payment order is a duplicate of the first or is another order. Similarly, in Case 1 and Case 2, the receiving bank may have no way of knowing that the error exists. In each case, if [§ 4A-205] does not apply and the funds transfer is completed, Sender is obliged to pay the order. Section 4A-402. Sender's remedy, based on payment by mistake, is to recover from the beneficiary that received payment.[78]

A different result may ensue, however, when the bank and the customer have agreed to use a security procedure to detect the customer's errors.

Sometimes, however, transmission of payment orders of the sender to the receiving bank is made pursuant to a security procedure designed to detect one or more of the errors described above. Since "security procedure" is defined by Section 4A-201 as "a procedure established by agreement of a customer and a receiving bank for the purpose of . . . detecting error . . . ," Section 4A-205 does not apply if the receiving bank and the customer did not agree to the establishment of a procedure for detecting error. A security procedure may be designed to detect an account number that is not one to which Sender normally makes payment. In that case, the security procedure may require a special verification that payment to the stated account number was intended. In the case of dollar amounts, the security procedure may require different codes for different dollar amounts. If a $1,000,000 payment order contains a code that is inappropriate for that amount, the error in amount should be detected. In the case of duplicate orders, the security procedure may require that each payment order be identified by a number or code that applies to no other order. If the number or code of each payment order received is registered in a computer base, the receiving bank can quickly identify a duplicate order.

When the bank and the customer have established a security procedure for the detection of the customer's errors and the conditions of § 4A-205 have been satisfied, liability for the customer's error may be shifted from the customer to the bank. The conditions are:

- The customer's payment order complies with the security procedure,
- The bank fails to comply with the procedure, and
- The customer proves that error would have been detected if the bank had complied with the procedure.

The Article 4A drafters seem to have believed that if a security procedure for the detection of the customer's errors has been established, the bank should comply with the procedure and assume liability for its failure to comply with it. Compliance with the procedure offers the parties a "last clear chance" to avoid the loss:

> . . . [T]he bank undertakes a duty of complying with the procedure for the benefit of the sender. This duty is recognized in [§ 4A-205(a)(1). The loss with respect to the sender's error is shifted to the bank if the bank fails to comply with the procedure and the sender (or an agent under Section 4A-206) does comply. Although the customer may have been negligent in transmitting the erroneous payment order, the loss is put on the bank on a last-clear-chance theory.[79]

If the conditions of § 4-05(a) have been satisfied and a loss is sustained as a result of an error in which funds are transferred to the wrong person or in an amount in excess of the amount intended by the customer or a duplicate order is erroneously executed, liability for the loss is shifted to the bank. In that event, the customer is relieved of the obligation to pay for the order except to the extent that the payment was not erroneous:

> In the case of a duplicate order or wrong beneficiary, the sender does not have to pay the order. In the case of an overpayment, the sender does not have to pay the order to the extent of the overpayment.[80]

However, liability for the order may shift back to the customer if the customer fails to notify the bank of the erroneous transfer. The customer has a duty to exercise "ordinary care,"[81] upon receipt of a bank statement or other notice that the erroneous payment order was executed by the bank, to discover the error and to report it to the bank within a reasonable time, not exceeding 90 days after receipt of the notice. If the bank proves that the customer failed to perform that duty, the customer becomes liable to the bank for the loss that the bank proves it incurred as a result of the customer's failure to comply with the duty. In other words, the loss that was shifted from the customer to the bank because the bank failed to comply with the security procedure may shift back to the customer if the customer fails to give the bank notice of the bank's execution of the erroneous payment order. The shift will occur only if the bank can demonstrate that the loss would have been prevented if the notice had been given:

> If the loss with respect to an error is shifted to the receiving bank and the sender is notified by the bank that the erroneous payment order was accepted, the sender has a duty to exercise ordinary care to discover the error and notify the bank of the relevant facts within a reasonable time not exceeding 90 days. If the bank can prove that the sender failed in this duty, it is entitled to compensation for the loss incurred as a result of the failure. Whether the bank is entitled to recover from the sender depends upon whether the failure to give timely notice would have made any difference. If the bank could not have recovered from the beneficiary that received payment under the erroneous payment order even if timely notice had been given, the sender's failure to notify did not cause any loss of the bank.[82]

Banks generally have not wished to be liable for their customers' errors, even when they fail to comply with security procedures for the detection of errors. Thus, wire transfer agreements between banks and their customers typically disclaim § 4A-205 liability for such errors:

> Section 4A-205 is subject to variation by agreement under Section 4A-501.[83] Thus, if a receiving bank and its customer have agreed to a security procedure for detection of error, the liability of the receiving bank for failing to

detect an error of the customer as provided in Section 4A-205 may be varied as provided in an agreement of the bank and its customer.[84]

Normally, a bank will want to disclaim liability under § 4A-205 in a wire transfer agreement. The disclaimer should be direct and unambiguous. A statement that there are no security procedures in effect for the detection of errors is not as effective as a statement disclaiming liability.

Reminder: Most risks of the wire transfer payment system are best controlled before the wire transfer order is released by the originator to its bank. Preventing and correcting errors are very difficult thereafter.

ENDNOTES

1. U.C.C. § 4A-212.
2. U.C.C. § 4A-209(b)(1)(i).
3. U.C.C. § 4A-405(a).
4. *Id.* In addition, if the bank does not credit an account of the beneficiary, the time when payment occurs is governed by "principles of law that determine when an obligation is satisfied." Under U.C.C. § 4A-405(b), an over-the-counter payment to the beneficiary would be governed by such legal principles. Such payment would constitute payment and acceptance under U.C.C. §§ 4A-405(b) and 4A-209(b)(1).
5. Official Comment 2 to U.C.C. § 4A-405.
6. U.C.C. § 4A-405(d).
7. U.C.C. § 4A-405(e).
8. U.C.C. § 4A-209(b)(1)(ii).
9. A person "notifies" another person under U.C.C. § 1-201(26) by taking such steps as may be reasonably required to inform the other person in the ordinary course, whether or not the other person actually comes to know of it.
10. Official Comment 5 to U.C.C. § 4A-209.

11. U.C.C. § 4A-209(b)(2).
12. Official Comment 6 to U.C.C. § 4A-209.
13. *Id.*
14. U.C.C. § 4A-401.
15. Official Comment 8 to U.C.C. § 4A-209.
16. U.C.C. § 4A-209(b)(3).
17. Official Comment 8 to U.C.C. § 4A-209. The notice must be given, at the latest, within one hour after the opening of the funds-transfer business day of the beneficiary's bank or the sender, whichever is later. Interest is computed on the basis of the *time of receipt* of the notice, not according to when it is sent. The extra days of delay beyond the one day presumably refer to notice in writing that is not received until a subsequent day and possibly not until after a weekend.
18. See Official Comment 4 to U.C.C. § 4A-211.
19. U.C.C. § 4A-211(c)(2).
20. Official Comment 4 to U.C.C. § 4A-211.
21. U.C.C. § 4A-404(a). The provision is subject to the Article 4A rules regarding cancellation of an accepted payment order (U.C.C. § 4A-211(e)) and funds transfer system rules (U.C.C. § 4A-405(d) and (e)).
22. *Id.*
23. *Id.* The rules regarding the availability of the funds under Article 4A may be subject to preemption by the Expedited Funds Availability Act, 12 U.S.C. 4001 *et seq.* See Official Comment 1 to U.C.C. § 4A-404. For a thoughtful discussion of such preemption, see Geva, *The Law of Electronic Funds Transfers,* 2.11[3].
24. U.C.C. § 4A-404(a).
25. U.C.C. § 4A-404(c).
26. 673 F.2d 951 (7th Cir. 1982).
27. Official Comment 2 to U.C.C. § 4A-404.
28. Official Comment 3 to U.C.C. § 4A-404.
29. U.C.C. § 4A-404(b).
30. Official Comment 4 to U.C.C. § 4A-404.
31. U.C.C. § 4A-404(a).

Endnotes

32. U.C.C. § 4A-406(b).
33. Official Comment 1 to U.C.C. § 4A-406.
34. Official Comment 2 to U.C.C. § 4A-406.
35. Official Comment 3 to U.C.C. § 4A-406.
36. See the last sentence of U.C.C. § 4A-406(b) for the originator's subrogation rights against Bank B.
37. U.C.C. § 4A-406(c).
38. U.C.C. § 4A-204(a).
39. U.C.C. § 4A-209(b)(3).
40. U.C.C. § 4A-210(b).
41. U.C.C. § 4A-305(a).
42. U.C.C. § 4A-402(d).
43. U.C.C. § 4A-404(b).
44. U.C.C. § 4A-506(a).
45. U.C.C. § 4A-506(b).
46. *Id.* Banks are required to deposit with the Federal Reserve a percentage of their deposits as a reserve requirement. The deposits do not earn interest.
47. Official Comment 1 to U.C.C. § 4A-506.
48. U.C.C. § 4A-504(a).
49. U.C.C. § 4A-507(b).
50. U.C.C. § 4A-507(a).
51. U.C.C. § 4A-502(b).
52. Specifically, with respect to the customer's errors, U.C.C. § 4A-302(a)(1) states that the receiving bank must issue a payment order complying with the sender's order.
53. U.C.C. §§ 4A-209(a), 4A-210(a), and 4A-212. Under U.C.C. § 4A-212, the receiving bank has no duty to accept a payment order or "before acceptance, to take any action, or refrain from taking action" with respect to the order except to the extent the bank has expressly agreed otherwise.
54. U.C.C. § 4A-207(b)(1).
55. *Id.*
56. Comment 2 to U.C.C. § 4A-207.
57. U.C.C. § 4A-207(c)(2).
58. Official Comment 3 to U.C.C. § 4A-207.

59. Comment 3 to U.C.C. § 4A-207.
60. U.C.C. § 4A-207(c)(2). For an example of a notice under § 4A-207, see § 2.3.1 of the American Bar Association's Model Funds Transfer Services Agreement. The notice is reproduced and U.C.C. § 4A-207 is discussed in Turner, *Negotiating Wire Transfer Agreements,* 19.
61. U.C.C. § 4A-207(b)(2).
62. U.C.C. § 4A-207(b)(1).
63. U.C.C. § 1-201(27) of Article 1. Article 1 contains general rules and definitions applicable to all of the Articles of the Uniform Commercial Code.
64. U.C.C. § 4A-207 (b)(1). See the discussion in Turner, *Negotiating Wire Transfer Agreements,* 21, in which it is suggested, wrongly, the author now believes, that the bank is more vulnerable to a claim that it failed to exercise due diligence when the funds transfer is a "book transfer," that is, when the originator and the beneficiary use the same bank.
65. Official Comment 2 to U.C.C. § 4A-207.
66. *Id.*
67. U.C.C. § 4A-207(d)(1). Mutual Fund would not seem to have an action against Doe, who would seem entitled to rescind the redemption, or against Roe if Roe is an innocent party, but Mutual Fund's rights against the wrongdoer, Doe, and Roe would be governed by law other than the law of U.C.C. Article 4A and are beyond the scope of this book.
68. Official Comment 2 to U.C.C. § 4A-208.
69. U.C.C. § 4A-305(b).
70. U.C.C. § 4A-208(b)(2). An originator that is not a bank is not entitled to the notice and could not hold the receiving bank liable for a breach of § 4A-302.
71. U.C.C. § 4A-208(b)(2).
72. The notice is reproduced and U.C.C. § 4A-208 discussed in Turner, *Negotiating Wire Transfer Agreements,* 19, 21.
73. U.C.C. § 4A-208(3).
74. U.C.C. § 4A-207(b)(2) provides that in the event of such wrongful payment, "acceptance of the order cannot occur."

The customer would accordingly be entitled to the benefit of the "money-back guarantee" provisions of U.C.C. § 4A-402. See Chapter 4.

75. The omission is probably an oversight and may be attributed to the fact that it is most unlikely that a bank would execute the customer's order with knowledge that the name and number identify different persons unless it also knew that the name or number in the bank's order to the next bank in the funds-transfer chain identified the right person. Even when the name and number identify different persons, the likelihood of loss resulting from the error seems minimal.

76. U.C.C. § 4A-208(b)(1).

77. Official Comment 1 to U.C.C. § 4A-205.

78. *Id.*

79. Official Comment 2 to U.C.C. § 4A-205.

80. Official Comment 1 to U.C.C. § 4A-205. See U.C.C. § 4A-205(a)(i) through (iii).

81. Article 4A does not define "ordinary care." For purposes of negotiable instrument law, that is, checks, U.C.C. § 3-103(a)(7) defines ordinary care as the observance of reasonable commercial standards.

82. Comment 2 to U.C.C. § 4A-205.

83. U.C.C. § 4A-501(a) provides that any provision of Article 4A may be varied by the agreement of the parties "except as otherwise provided" in Article 4A. Inasmuch as no provision forbids variation of U.C.C. § 4A-205, the bank may disclaim liability for the customer's errors under that section.

84. Comment 3 to U.C.C. § 4A-205.

6

Risks of Automated Clearing House Payments

The automated clearing house (ACH) payment system has operated under a system of rules that are accepted by all participants and have been in use for many years.

OVERVIEW

Business establishments use ACH transactions for many types of payments. Businesses pay bills owed to other businesses through ACH. Businesses originate consumer credits by paying employees direct deposits of payroll, reimbursements for travel, and benefits. They initiate consumer debits to re-present checks that have been returned for insufficient funds and to convert consumer checks presented at the point of purchase or mailed to a merchant or lockbox. Businesses receive ACH payments from purchasers of their goods and services. The success of the ACH payment system can be measured by its infrequent failures and invulnerability to the usual attempts at fraud.

The National Automated Clearing House Association (NACHA) is a nonprofit membership organization with about 40 regional member ACH associations that represent more than 12,000 financial institutions, which, in turn, provide ACH services to more than 3,500,000 companies and to more than 100 million consumers. NACHA sponsors the the Bankers Electronic Data Interchange (EDI) Council, the Electronic Check Council, the Bill Payment Council, the Cross-Border Council, the Electronic Benefits Transfer Council, the Internet Council and other councils, which oversee the rules and suggest changes and new rules for consideration by NACHA.

NACHA's stated purpose is "to develop and promote the national exchange of electronic entries among participating financial institutions."[1] For such an exchange to function effectively, a high degree of mutual understanding and cooperation among the individual participants is necessary, and the Operating Rules are designed to promote such a culture.[2] The ACH Operating Rules are issued annually by NACHA.

DEFINITIONS

There are two types of ACH transfers: a "credit" transfer and a "debit" transfer. In a *credit transfer*, the original instructions to make the transfer are given by the payor, the entity paying the funds. In a *debit transfer*, the instructions are given by the payee, the entity receiving the funds.

More precisely, in ACH terminology: In a "credit" transfer, funds are paid by the *payor* (the *Originator*) to the receiving *payee* (the *Receiver*). In a credit transaction, it is often said that funds are "pushed" from the account of the Originator into the account of the Receiver. The transfer is originated by the Originator instructing its bank, the *Originating Depository Financial Institution* (the ODFI), to make the transfer. The ODFI then instructs the ACH Operator to make the transfer. The instructions to the ACH Operator are routed through the processing facility of the Federal Reserve System in East Rutherford, New Jersey.

The ACH Operator is typically a Federal Reserve Bank, but if there is a private sector Operator in the region, the ODFI may choose to send the instructions to the private sector Operator instead of to the Federal Reserve Bank in the region. The ACH Operator advises the *Receiving Depository Financial Institution* (RDFI) of the transaction, and the RDFI notifies the Receiver and makes the funds available to the Receiver.

ACH credit transfers are governed by U.C.C. Article 4A except when any part of the transfer affects the account of a consumer. Consumer transfers are governed by the Electronic Fund Transfer Act (EFTA) and Regulation E, issued under EFTA by the Federal Reserve Board. The ACH Rules are designed to harmonize with the rules of Article 4A and Regulation E. ACH debit transfers are not governed by U.C.C. Article 4A, but under the ACH Rules, a debit entry is deemed an "item" under U.C.C. Article 4, the uniform law on checks and other negotiable instruments, and Article 4 applies to debit transfers except where its application is inconsistent with the ACH Rules.

Every Federal Reserve District is an ACH region. The ACH regional associations have typically employed the Federal Reserve Banks in their regions as the ACH Operators for transactions originating in the regions. There are, however, three private sector ACH Operators: (1) the Electronic Payments Network (EPN), an affiliate of the New York Automated Clearinghouse, (2) the American Clearinghouse Association in Phoenix, Arizona, and (3) VisaNet, which is owned by Visa, U.S.A. and operates for the most part in the Twelfth Federal Reserve District. Although private sector Operators have participated in a relatively small number of ACH transfers historically, EPN (which is owned by major money-center banks) has in recent years acted as the ACH Operator in a significant number of transfers.

Exhibit 6.1 provides a credit transfer illustration.

In a debit transfer, the flow of funds is the reverse of the flow in a credit transfer. It is often said that funds are "pulled" from the account of the Receiver into the account of the Originator. For

Exhibit 6.1 ACH Credit Transfer

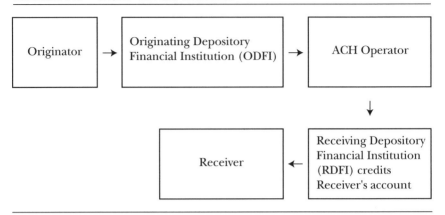

example, an insurance company may pull funds from the account of a policyholder to pay premiums on the policy. As in a credit transfer, the Originator instructs the ODFI, the ODFI instructs the ACH Operator, and the ACH Operator instructs the RDFI. However, instead of making funds available to the Receiver, the RDFI debits the account of the Receiver. Thus, in a debit transfer, the funds flow from the Receiver's account into the Originator's account.

A debit transfer is illustrated in Exhibit 6.2.

When the transfer is an interregional transfer, that is, out of one Federal Reserve District into another District, the ACH Operator that receives the instructions from the ODFI sends its instructions to the Federal Reserve Bank acting as the ACH Operator in the district of the RDFI.

An interregional credit transfer is illustrated in Exhibit 6.3; the ACH Operator in the region where the transfer originates is a Federal Reserve Bank. The instructions from the ODFI in the case of the transfers shown in Exhibits 6.1, 6.2, and 6.3 are routed through the Federal Reserve System processing facility in East Rutherford, New Jersey.

ORIGINATION OF ACH ENTRIES

Article 2 of the ACH Rules establishes the prerequisites for originating an ACH entry, the warranties and liabilities of "originat-

Exhibit 6.2   ACH Debit Transfer

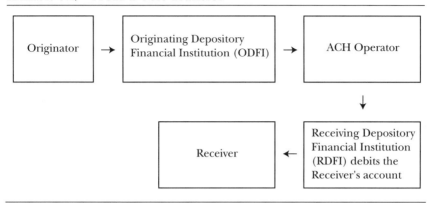

Exhibit 6.3   Interregional ACH Credit Transfer

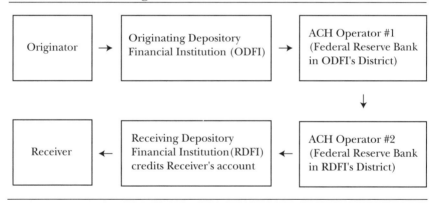

ing depository financial institutions" (ODFIs), and other provisions about the origination of entries. Article 3 of the Rules states the obligations of originators.

Prerequisites to Origination.   Before an Originator may initiate the first credit or debit entry to a Receiver or to a Receiver's account with a receiving depository financial institution (RDFI), the ACH Rules require the participants to comply with the following prerequisites to origination.

145

Authorization and Agreement by the Originator and the Receiver. Both the Originator and the Receiver must authorize the transfers. The Originator's authorization is given to the ODFI and the Receiver's to the Originator.

The Originator authorizes the ODFI "to transmit, and to credit or debit the amount of, one or more entries to the Receiver's account."[3] The rule also requires the Originator to be bound by the ACH Rules and to acknowledge that entries may not be initiated that violate the laws of the United States.[4]

The Receiver authorizes the Originator to initiate the entry to the Receiver's account.[5] In the case of corporate **cash concentration or disbursement (CCD)** entries or **corporate trade exchange (CTX)** entries, the Receiver must have an agreement with the Originator under which the Receiver agrees to be bound by the ACH Rules as in effect from time to time.[6]

In order for a business Originator to use ACH payments for charges to a consumer Receiver account, the authorization must be in writing and signed or "similarly authenticated." "Similarly authenticated" means that the authorization may be provided electronically. The ACH Rules provide generally that where any agreement, authorization, statement, or other kind of record must be in writing or must be signed, the record may be in electronic form and the signature may be an electronic signature if the record or the signature is in conformity with the federal Electronic Signatures in Global and Electronic Commerce Act (ESign).[7] In regard to the authorization by a consumer to the Originator of a debit entry to the consumer's account, the rules incorporate ESign and state that electronic signatures include the use of a digital signature or other security code.[8] The rule that an authorization must be in writing may be satisfied by the visual display of writing on a monitor or screen. The Receiver consumer account being debited may revoke the authorization by notifying the Originator recipient only in the manner specified in the authorization.[9]

There are important exceptions to the general rule that a consumer must affirmatively assent—in writing or in an electronic record "similarly authenticated"—to the origination of debit entries to the consumer's account. The exceptions include the authorization of RCK (re-presented checks), ARC (accounts receivable), and TEL (telephone-initiated) debit entries.

In an RCK entry, the merchant creates a debit to the consumer's account when the consumer's check has been returned for insufficient funds. In an ARC entry, the merchant converts a consumer's check received through the mail into an ACH debit entry to the consumer's account. The rules require that for RCK and ARC entries, the Originator must provide a notice to the consumer that by providing the check, the consumer authorizes the merchant to initiate a debit entry to the consumer's account.[10] In the case of TEL entries, in which the authorization is transmitted over the telephone, the authorization is oral, of course, but the rules specify the information that must be provided to the consumer and require the Originator to tape-record the authorization or provide the consumer with a written notice confirming the oral authorization.[11]

The Originator is required to provide the Receiver with an electronic or hard copy of the Receiver's authorization for debit entries. In the case of an RCK entry, the Originator must retain the original check for at least seven years after the date funds are exchanged as reflected in the books of the Federal Reserve banks. In the case of an ARC entry, the Originator must retain the original check for a 90-day period and a copy for two years. In addition, the Originator must retain the original, a microfilm, or an equivalent record of each written authorization given to the Originator by the Receiver for two years after the termination or revocation of the authorization. At the request of the ODFI, the Originator is required to provide that original or copy of it to the ODFI.[12] The record keeping rule does not apply, however, to machine terminal (MTE) or shared network (SHR) entries if the ODFI and the RDFI are parties to an agreement for the provision of services relating to such entries. The RDFI is not required to keep a file of authorizations and may, in writing, request a copy of the authorization from the ODFI.[13]

Notices from the ODFI to the Originator before the First ACH Entry. Certain notices must also be given as prerequisites to the Originator's initiating the first entry to a Receiver's account with an RDFI. These notices are derived from requirements in U.C.C. Article 4A.

ACH Rule 2.1.5 provides that in the case of a credit entry subject to U.C.C. Article 4A, the ODFI must have provided the Originator with notice of the following:

- The entry may be transmitted through the ACH system,
- The rights and obligations of the Originator will be governed by New York State law unless the Originator and ODFI have agreed on a different jurisdictional law,
- The credit given by the RDFI to the Receiver is provisional until the RDFI has received final payment, and
- If the RDFI does not receive final payment for the entry, the RDFI is entitled to a refund from the Receiver in the amount of the credit to the Receiver's account, and the Originator will not be considered to have paid the amount of the entry to the Receiver.[14]

These notices may be included as part of an ACH agreement between the Originator and the ODFI or provided by the ODFI to the Originator separately. The notices required from the ODFI to the Originator are important to managing the risk of ACH system participation.[15] Thus, the ACH payment rules are linked to U.C.C. Article 4A.

The U.C.C. Article 4A provisions make the payment of the beneficiary by the beneficiary's bank final. Article 4A allows a funds-transfer system to enact a rule that makes the payments provisional—but this rule requires that before the funds transfer is initiated, both the beneficiary Receiver and the payment Originator be given notice of the provisional nature of the payment. In addition, the Receiver beneficiary's bank and the Originator's bank, as well as the Receiver beneficiary, must have agreed to be bound by this provisional payment rule.[16]

ACH Rule 4.4.6 provides for the provisional nature of credit given to the Receiver by the RDFI with respect to any credit entry subject to U.C.C. Article 4A. If the RDFI has not received payment for the credit entry, the RDFI is entitled to a refund and the "Originator is considered not to have paid the Receiver the amount of the entry." ACH Rule 4.4.6 applies, however, only if the Receiver agrees to be bound by the Rule.

Thus, the prerequisite notices solve an ACH payment system risk as to provisional payments by linking ACH Rule 2.1.5 to implement ACH Rule 4.4.6 in accordance with U.C.C. § 4A-405(d). Put another way, ACH Rule 4.4.6 contains the rule that provides that the credits are provisional, and ACH Rule 2.1.5 provides for the notices that make Rule 4.4.6 effective pursuant to U.C.C. § 4A-405(d).

Notices from the RFDI to the Receiver before the First ACH Entry. Similarly, ACH Rule 2.1.6 requires as a prerequisite to the origination by an Originator of a credit entry subject to U.C.C. Article 4A that the RDFI give the following notices to the Receiver:

- The entry may be transmitted through the ACH system,
- The rights and obligations of the Receiver will be governed by the law of the State of New York unless the Receiver and the RDFI have agreed on a different jurisdictional law,
- Credit given by the RDFI to the Receiver is provisional until the RDFI has received final settlement, and
- If the RDFI does not receive payment for the entry, the RDFI is entitled to a refund from the Receiver, and the Originator will not be considered to have paid the amount of the credit entry to the Receiver.

The foregoing notices complete the implementation of the provisional rule consistent with the requirements of Article 4A by requiring that notices similar to those given to the Receiver under ACH Rule 2.1.5 be given to the Receiver under ACH Rule 2.5.6.

ODFI Exposure Limits for Business Originators. Rule 2.1.9 requires the ODFI to maintain exposure limits for all Originators that are not natural persons. If the Originator is a corporation or other nonnatural business entity, the ODFI is obliged to establish the limit, to implement procedures to review the limit periodically, and to implement procedures to monitor entries initiated by the Originator relative to the exposure limit. Additional exposure limit requirements are imposed on initiators of web entries, who are required to use commercially reasonable security procedures to establish the identity of the Originator.

Warranties and Liabilities of the ODFI

What Is a Warranty? A warranty is a representation that a statement of fact is true or that circumstances are what they ought to be. There are two kinds of warranties: contractual warranties and statutory warranties.

A contractual warranty is provided voluntarily by a party to a contract. The kind of warranty that is commonly termed a *manufacturer's warranty* is contractual. Thus, when a consumer buys a refrigerator, the manufacturer may warrant in a warranty card to the consumer that the refrigerator will not require any service or repair for a period of two years. If the refrigerator breaks down within the two-year period, the manufacturer is in breach of warranty and may be sued for that breach unless the refrigerator is repaired according to the terms of the warranty.

A *statutory warranty* is imposed on a party by statute. For example, a grantor of real estate pursuant to a warranty deed is deemed under state real property law to warrant that good title is transferred to the grantee.

ODFI's Contractual Warranties under ACH Rules. The ACH Rules are funds-transfer system rules and do not have the force of statutory law. The warranties that are deemed given by the parties under the ACH Rules are contractual because the parties voluntarily agree by contract to be bound by the ACH Rules.

The ODFI is deemed to give the warranties to the RDFI, the ACH Operator, and the member associations of NACHA. As a general proposition, the warranties assure the RDFI, the ACH Operator, and the member associations that the ODFI will be responsible for claims asserted by either the Originator or the Receiver arising out of alleged improprieties in the underlying transaction.

ODFI Warrants Authorization By Originator and Receiver. The ODFI warrants to the RDFI, the ACH Operator, and the member associations of NACHA that each entry transmitted by the ODFI to the ACH Operator is in accordance with proper authorization provided by the Originator and the Receiver.[17] Stated differently, the ODFI agrees that if the transfer has not been properly authorized and a loss results—as between the beneficiaries of the warranty, that is, the RDFI, the ACH Operator, and the member associations of NACHA, and the warrantor, the ODFI—the ODFI will be liable to the party asserting a claim to recover the loss.

The result is that the ODFI indemnifies the RDFI, the ACH Operator, and the member associations for losses resulting from claims by the Originator or the Receiver that a transfer was not authorized.

Note: The ODFI is not agreeing with the Originator or the Receiver to pay for losses that they may sustain when a transfer is not properly authorized. Rather, the ODFI is agreeing—with the RDFI, the ACH Operator, and the member associations—to shoulder any claims arising out of allegedly unauthorized transfers asserted against them by the Originator or the Receiver.

ODFI Warranty about Timeliness and Propriety of Entries. The ODFI warrants to the RDFI, the ACH Operator, and the member associations that each entry is authorized and[18]:

(i) each credit entry is timely, and
(ii) each debit entry is
    (a) for an amount that will be owing to the Originator from the Receiver on the settlement date, and

(b) for a sum specified by the Receiver to be paid to the Originator (or to correct a previously transmitted erroneous credit entry).

In these warranties, the ODFI is indemnifying the RDFI, the ACH Operator, and the member associations from claims asserted by the Originator and the Receiver in the underlying transaction. As in the preceding warranty, the ODFI is not agreeing with the Originator or the Receiver to pay for losses that they may sustain when a payment is not timely or not properly payable. Rather, the ODFI is agreeing—with the RDFI, the ACH Operator, and the member associations—to shoulder any claims arising out of an allegedly improper payment asserted against them by the Originator or the Receiver.

ODFI Warranty about Compliance with Other Requirements. The ODFI warrants to the RDFI, the ACH Operator, and the member associations that[19]:

  (i) all of the prerequisites under ACH Rule 2.1 concerning authorization and entry have been satisfied,
 (ii) the entry has not been reinitiated contrary to the ACH Rules,[20] and
(iii) the entry otherwise complies with the ACH Rules.

ODFI Warranty about Revocation of Authorizations. At the time the entry is transmitted to the Originating ACH Operator[21]:

  (i) the Originator's authorization has not been revoked,
 (ii) the agreement between the ODFI and the Originator concerning the entry has not been terminated, and
(iii) neither the ODFI nor the Originator has actual knowledge of the revocation of the Receiver's authorization or of the termination of the arrangement between the RDFI and the Receiver concerning the entry.

ODFI Warranty about Termination of Authorization by Operation of Law. At the time the entry is processed by the RDFI, the authorization for the entry has not been terminated in whole or in part by operation of law.[22]

ODFI Warranty about PIN Requirements. If a **personal identification number (PIN)** is required for a machine terminal (MTE), point of sale (POS), or shared network (SHR) entry, the Originator has complied with the applicable American National Standards Institute (ANSI) requirements.[23]

ODFI Warranty about Transmittal of Required Information. Each entry transmitted by the ODFI to the ACH Operator contains the correct Receiver account number and other information necessary to enable the RDFI to comply with the ACH Rules relating to the furnishing of Periodic Statements,[24] except for information within the purview of the RDFI's relationship with the Receiver. Information transmitted with the entry is payment related and conforms to the record format specifications of Appendix Two of the ACH Rules.

ODFI Warranty about Reclamation Entries for Governmental Benefits. If the purpose of the ACH transfers is to pay governmental benefits to the Receiver and the Receiver dies before the RDFI receives a payment, the RDFI may be liable for the return of the payment. Such payments are returned by the transmittal of a reclamation entry from the ODFI to the RDFI.[25] The ODFI warrants to the RDFI, the ACH Operator, and the member associations that[26]:

   (i)   the information in the entry is correct,
  (ii)   the entry is timely and properly authorized, and
 (iii)   any payment for which the RDFI is liable is not subject to restriction on the number of parties having an interest in the account at the RDFI.

ODFI Warranty about "Sending Points." A sending point is an entity that sends entries to the ACH Operator on behalf of the ODFI. If the entry is transmitted to the ACH Operator by a sending point, the ODFI warrants to the RDFI, the ACH Operator, and the member associations that the entry is transmitted pursuant to an agreement between the ODFI and the sending point.[27]

The ODFI warrants that it has complied with the audit requirements imposed on the ODFI by Appendix Eight of the ACH Rules.

Warranties about POP and TEL Entries. If the Originator is a merchant that has converted a consumer's check into a debit entry at the point of purchase (POP), the ODFI warrants that the original check has been returned voided to the consumer and has not been provided by the consumer for use in any prior POP entry. If the Originator has initiated a TEL entry, the ODFI warrants that the Originator has used commercially reasonable security procedures to verify the identity of the Receiver and to verify that routing numbers are valid.

Liability of ODFI for Breach of Warranty.[28] The ODFI has no liability in connection with a claim asserted by the Originator or the Receiver with respect to the goods or services.[29] The ODFI is otherwise broadly liable under ACH Rule 2.2.3.

What Is an Indemnity?

An indemnity is an agreement to hold an indemnified party harmless from claims by third parties. ACH Rule 2.2.3 requires the ODFI to indemnify the RDFI, the ACH Operator, and the member associations against claims and expenses, including attorney's fees and costs, resulting from a breach of warranty. This indemnity is even broader, because it covers claims and expenses resulting from "the debiting or crediting of the entry to the Receiver's account." Presumably, these are claims and expenses that would be based on the ground that the debiting of an entry to an account resulted in the return of items or entries due to insufficient funds. These are claims and expenses that are specifically included in the Rule 2.2.3 indemnity, which also includes, in the case of a consumer account, claims resulting from the RDFI's violation of **Regulation E**.

ACH Prenotification

Prenotification is an optional method of testing the efficacy of an ACH entry. Prior to initiating the first entry to a Receiver, the Originator may deliver or send notification (referred to by practitioners as a "prenote") through the ODFI to the ACH Operator for transmittal to the RDFI.[30] The prenotification must provide notice to the RDFI that the Originator intends to initiate one or more entries to the Receiver's account.

When the Originator has initiated a prenotification, the Originator must wait six banking days before initiating entries to the Receiver's account.[31] If, within the six-banking-day period, the RDFI has transmitted to its ACH Operator and the ODFI has received a return entry indicating that the RDFI will not accept the entries, the entries will not be initiated. If, within the six-banking-day period, the RDFI has transmitted to its ACH Operator and the ODFI has received a Notification of Change, the entries may be made only if they comply with the Notification of Change.[32] A Notification of Change is a notice by an RDFI instructing the ODFI to make a change in entries sent by the ODFI to the RDFI.[33]

Reversing Duplicate and Erroneous Files

The general rule under ACH Rule 2.4.1 allows the Originator, the ODFI, and the ACH Operator to initiate a file of reversing entries (referred to as a "reversing file") to reverse duplicate or erroneous files if no other right to recall the entries is available under the rules.[34]

A duplicate file is a file that is erroneously sent into the ACH system twice. Because duplicate files contain identical data, each

Receiver is erroneously credited (in a credit transfer) or debited (in a debit transfer) twice. An erroneous file under Rule 2.4.1 is one in which each entry or each entry in one or more **batches** contains erroneous data. An erroneous file may contain errors throughout the whole file, errors in a batch, or errors in a number of batches that are part of the file.

A reversing file must be initiated in time to be available to the RDFI within five banking days after the settlement date of the duplicate or erroneous file.[35] The "settlement date" is the date the exchange of funds, with respect to the entry, is to be reflected on the books of the Federal Reserve Bank.[36] The reversing file must be accompanied by a file that contains the correct information (referred to as a "correcting file").[37]

If a reversing file is initiated by the Originator or the ODFI, the file must be transmitted to the Originating ACH Operator within 24 hours of the discovery of the duplication or the error.[38] If a reversing file is initiated by the ACH Operator, it must be transmitted to the Receiving ACH Operator or RDFI within 24 hours of the discovery of the duplication or error.

If a reversing file is initiated by an ACH Operator, the Operator must give notice of the duplication or error at or prior to the initiation of the reversing file. If the ACH Operator is a Receiving ACH Operator, the notice is given to the Originating ACH Operator. If the ACH Operator is an Originating ACH Operator, the notice is given to the ODFI.[39]

The ODFI or ACH Operator that initiates a reversing file broadly indemnifies every participating depository financial institution from expenses and claims, including attorney's fees, resulting from the debiting or crediting of any entry in the reversing file to the Receiver's account. The ODFI also assumes responsibility for the Originator.[40] The ODFI indemnifies the RDFI, ACH Operator, and member associations from expenses and claims, including attorney's fees, resulting from the crediting or debiting of any entry contained in a reversing or correcting file initiated by the Originator through the ODFI.

The right of the Originator to reverse a duplicate or erroneous file is unqualified. It applies to credit, debit, consumer, and nonconsumer entries at the precompletion and postcompletion stages of payment. It does not, however, apply to single entries, and the ACH Rules impose a broad indemnification obligation on the party reversing payment. If that party is the Originator, the Rules impose the indemnification obligation on the ODFI.

Risk of Duplicate or Erroneous Files. The potential exposure arising from a duplicate or erroneous file can be very great. It appears that the drafters of the ACH Rules believed that the exposure warranted the erring party having an unqualified right—not conditional upon the RDFI's agreement, as is the case for a single erroneous completed payment entry—to reverse the file.[41] This unqualified right is balanced by the indemnity of the ODFI, not only for its own actions but also for the actions of the Originator.

Reversing Duplicate and Erroneous Entries

ACH Rule 2.5 applies to erroneous entries. For purposes of the Rule, an erroneous entry is an entry that:

- Is a duplicate of an entry previously initiated by an Originator or an ODFI,
- Orders payment to or from a Receiver not intended to be credited or debited by the Originator, or
- Orders payment in an amount different from that intended by the Originator.

The general rule under ACH Rule 2.5 permits the Originator to initiate an entry (referred to as a "reversing entry") to correct an erroneous debit or credit entry previously initiated to the Receiver's account.[42] The Originator must notify the Receiver of the reversing entry and the reasons for the entry not later than the settlement date. The "settlement date" is the date the exchange of funds, with respect to the entry, is to be reflected on the books of the Federal Reserve Bank.[43]

Unlike the rule with respect to reversing files,[44] the rule applicable to reversing entries states that *entries cannot be reversed after the settlement date.* The ODFI that initiates a reversing entry broadly indemnifies every participating depository financial institution from expenses and claims, including attorney's fees, resulting from the debiting or crediting of the reversing entry to the Receiver's account. The ODFI also assumes responsibility for the Originator.[45] The ODFI indemnifies the RDFI, ACH Operator, and member associations from expenses and claims, including attorney's fees, resulting from the crediting or debiting of the reversing entry initiated by the Originator through the ODFI.

Originating Destroyed Check Entries

A *cash letter* is a deposit of checks by a financial institution at another financial institution or at a Federal Reserve Bank. The checks contained within the cash letter are drawn on banks within the geographic area to which the cash letter is being sent. Often, a cash letter contains only checks drawn on the financial institution receiving the cash letter. If a check contained within a cash letter has been lost or destroyed or otherwise becomes unavailable while in transit for presentment to the paying bank, the ODFI may initiate a destroyed check XCK entry.[46]

To be eligible for a destroyed check entry, the check must be an item within the meaning of U.C.C. Article 4 and a "negotiable demand draft" (read about drafts in Chapter 3) "drawn on or payable through or at" an office of a participating depository financial institution other than a Federal Reserve Bank or Federal Home Loan Bank. In addition, the check must be in an amount that is less than $2,000. Noncash items, drafts drawn on the Treasury of the United States, drafts drawn on a state or local government that are not payable through or at a bank, United States Postal Service money orders, items payable in a medium other than United States money, return items, and items that are rejected during processing by the ODFI are not eligible.[47]

In addition to the regular ODFI warranties,[48] the ODFI initiating a destroyed check entry makes warranties that are similar to the warranties of a bank presenting a check.[49] The RDFI that receives the entry may return the entry under the regular provisions that govern the right of RDFIs to return entries.[50] In addition, the RDFI may return the entry to the ODFI by transmitting a return entry to its ACH Operator by midnight of the 60th day following the settlement date of the destroyed check entry.[51] If the RDFI sends the ODFI a request for a copy of the check within six years of the date of the destroyed check entry initiated by the ODFI, the ODFI must furnish the copy within 30 days.

Reinitiation of Returned Entries to Originators

After the RDFI has returned an entry to the ODFI, the Originator's right to reinitiate the entry is limited. The entry may be reinitiated only if it was returned for insufficient funds, payment was stopped and reinitiation is authorized by the Receiver, or the ODFI has taken corrective action to remedy the reason for the return. An entry that has been returned for insufficient funds may be reinitiated no more than twice following the return of the original entry.[52]

Miscellaneous Obligations of Originators

Record keeping requirement. As noted earlier, a prerequisite to origination is that the Receiver has authorized the Originator to initiate the entry to the Receiver's account.[53] ACH Rule 3.5 requires the Originator to retain the original or a microfilm equivalent copy of each authorization of a Receiver for two years after the termination or revocation of the authorization. If the ODFI requests the Originator to provide the original or copy for the use of the ODFI or of the RDFI, the Originator must comply with that request.[54]

Personal Identification Numbers. If a PIN is required to authorize a machine terminal (MTE), point of sale (POS), or shared network (SHR) entry, the Originator must comply with the ANSI requirements concerning PIN Management and Security.[55]

Preauthorized Debit Transfers from a Consumer's Account. In preauthorized debt transfers from a consumer's account, the consumer is the Receiver. The consumer authorizes the Originator, usually a business, to initiate debit transfers for payments from the consumer. If the amount of a debit entry to the consumer's account differs from the amount of the immediately preceding debit entry relating to the same authorization or differs from the preauthorized amount, the ACH Rules require the Originator to send the consumer written notification of the amount of the entry and the date on or after which the entry will be debited. The notice must be sent at least 10 calendar days prior to the date on which the entry is scheduled to be initiated.[56] However, if the Originator informs the consumer that the consumer has the right to receive notification of changes in the amount of the entries, the consumer may elect to receive notice only if the amount of the entry falls outside a specified range or if the entry differs from the most recent entry by more than an agreed amount.[57]

Moreover, the ACH Rules require the Originator to give notice to the consumer of a change in the date on or after which entries to be initiated by the Originator are scheduled to be debited to the consumer's account. The notice is to be sent within at least seven calendar days before the first entry to be affected by the change is scheduled to be debited to the consumer's account.[58]

Finally, the Originator must provide the consumer with an electronic or hard copy of the consumer's authorization for all debit entries to be initiated to the consumer's account.[59]

RECEIPT OF ENTRIES: RDFIs AND RECEIVERS

The discussion now turns to the other side of the ACH transactions—the Receiving Depository Financial Institutions (RDFIs) and the

Receivers. These are the entities that are receiving ACH payment transactions, either debits or credits. Reliably unbending ACH Rules are critical to minimizing ACH payments system risk. Thus, the ACH Rules bind the RDFI, but not to as many obligations as those that apply to the ODFI.

Rights and Obligations of RDFI. Before acting as an RDFI for a Receiver, an RDFI has a right to request in writing that the ODFI provide the RDFI with a copy of the Receiver's authorization for entries other than cash concentration and disbursement (CCD), corporate trade payment (CTX), and destroyed check (XCK) entry.[60] Upon receipt of the RDFI's request, the ODFI must obtain the original or a copy of the Receiver's authorization from the Originator. The RDFI may not require the Receiver to provide other information concerning the Receiver or entries to be initiated to the Receiver's account.[61]

An RDFI that receives a prenotification must verify that the account number contained in the prenotification is for a valid account. If the prenotification does not contain a valid account number or is otherwise erroneous or unprocessable, the RDFI must reject the prenotification and transmit a return entry.[62] The RDFI must accept prenotifications that comply with the ACH prenotification rules.[63]

If the name of the Receiver and the account number contained in an entry do not relate to the same account, the RDFI may rely solely on the account number.[64]

Warranties of RDFI. The RDFI warrants to the ODFI, ACH Operator, and the member ACH associations that it has the power under applicable law[65]:

- To receive entries as provided in the rules, and
- To comply with the requirements of the rules concerning RDFIs and other participating depository financial institutions.

161

An RDFI that breaches the warranty must indemnify the ODFI, ACH Operator, and member associations from expenses and claims, including attorney's fees, resulting from the breach.

Receipt and Availability of Entries

RDFI and Credit Entries. The RDFI has broad rights under ACH Rule 5.1 to return entries. Subject to these rights to reject and return entries, the RDFI must make the amount of a credit entry it receives from its ACH Operator available to the Receiver no later than the settlement date.[66] In the case of a consumer preauthorized credit entry that is made available[67] to an RDFI by its ACH Operator by 5:00 P.M. on the banking day prior to the settlement date, the entry must be made available to the consumer at the opening of business on the settlement date.[68]

Provisional Credit Rule for Businesses. The credit availability rules, however, are subject to the provisional credit rule. A credit entry that is subject to U.C.C. Article 4A—typically a business transaction—is provisional until the RDFI has received final payment through a Federal Reserve Bank or has otherwise received payment as provided in Article 4A.[69] If such settlement or payment is not received, the RDFI is entitled to a refund from the Receiver. In that event, the payment between the Receiver and its bank is reversed.

Under U.C.C. Article 4A, if a bank makes a payment that is provisional under the funds-transfer system rule, the bank is entitled to a refund under Article 4A if the following rules have been observed:

- Both the beneficiary and the originator have been given notice of the provisional nature of the payment—so businesses should be alert to any "provisional" payment notices,
- The beneficiary, the beneficiary's bank, and the originator's bank have agreed to be bound by the rule, and
- The beneficiary's bank has not received payment.

Debit Entries. In regard to debit entries, the RDFI may not debit the Receiver's account prior to the settlement date of the entry, even if the date on which the Originator expects payment to occur is different from the settlement date.[70] The settlement date is the date an exchange of funds, with respect to an entry, is reflected on the books of the Federal Reserve.[71]

Electronic Data Interchange (EDI) ACH Addenda Record. Payment-related information contained within the Addenda Records transmitted with cash concentration and disbursement (CCD), consumer initiated entry (CIE), and corporate trade payment (CTX) entries must be provided by the RDFI to the Receiver—if the Receiver requests the data.[72] An *addenda record* is a type of ACH record that carries supplemental data that is needed to identify the account holder or provide information concerning a payment to the RDFI or the Receiver. The information must be provided by the opening of business on the second banking day following the Settlement Date of the entry.

The purpose of the rule is to promote and encourage the use of EDI. At the time the rule was adopted, many smaller banks had declined to invest in the software and equipment necessary to provide EDI to their customers. Many business customers had not furnished EDI to their trading partners because their banks did not have the technological capabilities.

Notice and Periodic Statements to a Receiver. Some are surprised that an RDFI is not required under the ACH Rules to give notice to the Receiver of any receipt of an entry to the Receiver's account.[73] Only if the Receiver is a consumer is the RDFI required to furnish periodic statements to the Receiver.[74]

Unauthorized Debit Transfers. If funds are transferred out of a Receiver's account as a result of an unauthorized debit entry, the Receiver "shall have rights, including the right to have the account recredited as provided by law or agreement."[75]

What Rights Does the Receiver Have under Law? Article 4A is not available because it does not apply to debit transfers.

If the Receiver is a consumer, the Receiver has the rights afforded to consumers under the fraudulent transfer provisions of Regulation E.

If the Receiver is a business, check law is applicable. The ACH Rules provide that each debit entry shall be deemed an "item" within the meaning of Article 4 of the Uniform Commercial Code and that Article 4 will apply to such entries except where the application is inconsistent with these rules, in which case these rules will control. Checks are discussed in Chapter 3.

In other words, an ACH debit is treated as though it were a check. An unauthorized debit would thus be essentially similar to a forged check and not "properly payable" out of the Receiver's account.[76] The RDFI, however, would be able to assert the Receiver's failure to exercise ordinary care[77] and other defenses available to the bank against the customer in a forged check case.[78]

Receiver and Originator: Closing the Loop

ACH Rule 4.4.4 requires the Receiver either (1) to credit the account of the Originator, as of the settlement date, with the amount of the entry credited to the Receiver's account at the RDFI or (2) to return the entry to the RDFI. In either case, the Receiver has a reasonable period of time within which to act. For purposes of the Rule, the Receiver is considered to act within a reasonable period of time if the Receiver posts the credit to the Originator's account or returns the entry no later than the time when the Receiver would normally complete the process of posting credits to its customers' accounts or returning those payments.[79]

The Rule requires the Receiver timely to credit the Originator's account or return the payment—there is no third choice such as suspending the payment within the Receiver's accounting or banking reconciliation system. If the Receiver cannot timely identify and credit the Originator, it is required to return the payment.

RETURNS, CHANGES, AND ACKNOWLEDGMENTS

The general rule allows an RDFI to return an entry "for any reason." Also, the RDFI is required to return any entries that have not been made available to its Receivers' accounts by midnight of the banking day following the settlement date. Returns, changes, and acknowledgments are covered by ACH Rules 5.1 through 5.5.

The ACH Rule is that a timely return must be made available to the ODFI by the opening of business on the second banking day after the settlement date of the original entry.

For example, if the original entry is received by the RDFI on Monday for settlement on that day, the deadline for return is the opening of business on Wednesday, the second banking day following the settlement date (Monday) of the original entry.

Exceptions to the Two-Banking-Day Deadline for Returns

There are exceptions to the two-banking-day deadline for returns. First, if the return relates to a credit entry subject to U.C.C. Article 4A, it must be transmitted by the RDFI to its ACH Operator before the RDFI "accepts" the credit entry under the Article 4A rules.

Second, the Receiver may return a credit entry to the RDFI instead of posting the credit to the Originator's account. When the Receiver returns the unposted entry to the RDFI, the RDFI's deadline for returning the entry to the ACH Operator is midnight of the banking day following the banking day of receipt by the RDFI of the entry from the Receiver.

A third exception to the two-banking-day rule relates to the right of a Receiver who is a consumer to demand that the RDFI recredit the Receiver's account after the account has been debited pursuant to an ACH debit entry. In the case of debit entries other than ARC, POP, and RCK entries, the consumer invokes the recredit rights by giving notice to the RDFI that the debit entry was "not authorized." The notice must be given within 15 calendar days from the date the RDFI sends or makes available

165

to the Receiver the periodic statement disclosing the debit. "Not authorized" means that the general authorization rules under ACH Rule 2.1.2 have not been satisfied or either (1) the debit entry was in an amount greater than the authorized amount or (2) the debit entry was initiated earlier than was authorized.

In the case of a POP entry, the consumer must state in the 15-day notice that the debit entry was not authorized or that either (1) the check was not a proper source document under ACH Rule 3.7.1 or (2) the check was presented for payment.

In the case of ARC or RCK entries, authorization is not the issue, but the consumer must state generally that (1) the consumer did not receive notice that the consumer's check would be used to initiate a debit entry, (2) the consumer's check was not an appropriate source for conversion into a debit entry under the ACH Rules, (3) the check was presented for payment, or (4) the amount of the entry did not reflect the amount of the check.

Upon receipt of a notice as described earlier (or receipt of the consumer's notice that a stop payment order has been placed on the check used to initiate the debit entry), the RDFI must promptly recredit the consumer's account. The RDFI may then return the entry, and the deadline for return of the entry by the RDFI is the deposit deadline of the ACH Operator for the adjustment entry to be made available to the ODFI by the opening of business on the 60th calendar day following the settlement date of the original entry.

The deadlines for returns described here are all subject to the general rule that delays are excused when caused by circumstances beyond the control of the participating depository financial institutions so long as the institutions exercise such diligence as the circumstances require.[80]

An entry that has been returned may be reinitated if the entry has been returned for insufficient funds or because of a stop payment order with authorized reinitiation, or if the ODFI has taken corrective action to remedy the reason for the return.

Refusal to Accept Returned Entries ("Dishonor")

When the RDFI has returned an entry, the ODFI may accept the return or refuse to accept it. The ODFI may dishonor a return for the following reasons[81]:

- The ODFI can substantiate that the RDFI has failed to return the entry within the deadlines of the ACH Rules, or
- The return entry contained incorrect information or did not comply with the information or specification requirements of Appendix Five to the Rules.

To dishonor a return entry, the ODFI must transmit a dishonored return entry complying with the specification requirements within five banking days after the settlement date of the return entry.[82]

If the dishonor of the return entry is based on the return entry's containing incorrect information or not complying with the information or specification requirements of Appendix Five to the Rules, the RDFI may transmit a corrected return entry to its ACH Operator. The deadline for transmission of the corrected return entry is five banking days after the settlement date of the dishonored return entry. The ODFI must accept a contested dishonored return entry.

If the dishonor of the return entry is based on the return entry's having failed to comply with the ACH Rules' return entry deadline and the return entry was, in fact, returned within the deadline, the RDFI may contest the dishonor. The RDFI contests the dishonored return entry by initiating a contested dishonored return entry. The deadline for transmitting a contested dishonored return entry is two banking days after the settlement date of the dishonored return entry.[83]

The ODFI must accept a complying contested dishonored return entry transmitted by the RDFI[84] and may not contest the entry by reinitiating the entry. Any further action by the ODFI concerning such entries must be pursued by the parties to the ACH transaction outside the ACH Rules.[85]

The sequence and timing of original entry, return entry, and dishonored or contested return entries are shown in Exhibit 6.4.

Notification of Change

A notification of change (NOC) is a non-dollar entry sent by an RDFI to the ACH Operator for the Operator to send to the ODFI and the ODFI to send back to the Originator. The notification is created by the RDFI in response to the receipt by the RDFI of a prenotification or a dollar entry that contains incorrect information. The notification of change is supposed to identify the entry that has been received by the RDFI, pinpoint the information that is incorrect, and provide the correct information in a precise format so that the Originator can make the change.

Exhibit 6.4 Sequence and Timing of ACH Original Entry, Return Entry, and Dishonored or Contested Return Entries

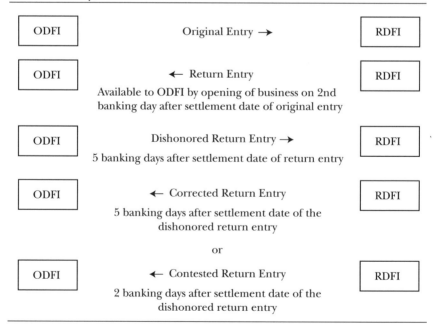

To refuse an NOC, the ODFI must transmit an automated refused notification of change within 15 days of receipt of the NOC (or corrected NOC). The RDFI may transmit a corrected NOC to the Receiving ACH Operator within five banking days after the settlement date of the refused notification of change.

Unless the ODFI refuses the NOC as described here within the 15-day period, the ODFI must accept the NOC and "at a minimum," must provide to the Originator information relating to the NOC in accordance with the requirements of Appendix Six.[86] The Originator must make the changes specified in the NOC (or corrected NOC) within six banking days or prior to initiating another entry to the Receiver's account, whichever is later.

Acknowledgments

An acknowledgment entry is a non-dollar transaction transmitted by the RDFI in response to a request for an acknowledgment contained in a cash concentration and disbursement (CCD) or corporate trade exchange (CTX) entry. The acknowledgment verifies that a corporate entry has been received by the RDFI. An acknowledgment entry must be received by the RDFI's ACH Operator by the Operator's deadline for the acknowledgment entry to be available to the ODFI no later than the opening of business on the second banking day following the settlement date of the CCD or CTX entry to which the acknowledgment relates.[87]

Note: The acknowledgment is an acknowledgment that the RDFI has received the entry and does not indicate that funds have been received by the Receiver.

SETTLEMENT AND ACCOUNTABILITY

The clearing and settlement of nongovernment ACH transactions is governed by Uniform Operating Circular No. 4 issued by the Federal Reserve Banks. In this context, an "Operating Circular" is a contract between a depository institution and its Federal Reserve Bank.[88] The Circular states that it governs the "clearing and settlement of commercial automated clearing house (ACH) credit and debit items (including credit items subject to Article 4A) by the Federal Reserve Banks, sending banks, and receiving banks."[89] The Circular incorporates U.C.C. Article 4A.[90] It also incorporates the ACH Rules and the Operating Rules of the regional ACH associations to the extent that the rules bind the sending and receiving institutions or generally apply to transactions in the region where the institutions are located.[91]

The following case is an example of a distinction between the check rules of U.C.C. Articles 3 and 4 and the ACH Rules. In *Sinclair Oil Corporation v. Sylvan State Bank*,[92] Sinclair was the Originator and Sinclair's bank was the ODFI. Sinclair's bank debited the account of a distributor of Sinclair's oil products at Sylvan State Bank, the RDFI. Sylvan returned the item by its midnight deadline, under the check law rules of U.C.C. Article 4, at midnight on the following day. The return would have been timely under U.C.C. Article 4,[93] but not timely under the ACH Rules. The ACH Rules require a return entry to be received by the RDFI's ACH Operator by its deposit deadline for the return entry to be made available to the ODFI no later than the opening of business on the second day following the settlement date of the original entry.[94] That deadline was 2:00 P.M. at the Federal Reserve Bank in Kansas City, and Sylvan's return entry was not in time to meet it.

Paragraph 1 of Operating Circular No. 12 of the Federal Reserve Bank in Kansas City stated that the Circular was binding on originators, receivers, and other parties interested in an item and on each account holder agreeing to settle for items under that letter.

The issue was whether Sinclair had standing to assert the NACHA rules. Sinclair was not an "account holder," a term that applies to banks that have accounts at the Federal Reserve Banks. Was Sinclair a party "interested in an item"? The court held that it was an issue of fact whether Sinclair was a party by agreement to the NACHA rules. Under ACH Rule 2.1.1, it is a prerequisite to origination that the Originator and the ODFI enter into an agreement to be bound by the rules. There was evidence that such an agreement between Sinclair and its bank had been entered into. The court seems to have concluded that under the Operating Circular, Sinclair had standing to assert the NACHA rules as a contracting party to the rules if it could show that the agreement existed. Therefore, the return was not timely and Sinclair still had the benefit of the ACH payment.

Security Procedures

Before transmitting an entry to a Reserve Bank as its ACH Operator, a sending financial institution must execute an agreement with the Reserve Bank in the form of Appendix A of the Circular. Under the Circular, the institution is "deemed to agree to any security procedure used in sending an item to a Reserve Bank."[95] Sending and receiving institutions are also required to prevent disclosure, except on a "need to know" basis, of aspects of the security procedures, to notify the Federal Reserve Bank if the confidentiality of the security procedures is compromised, and to act to prevent the security procedures from being further compromised.[96]

The "Level One Security Procedure" is available to any bank that issues or receives ACH items by means of an encrypted leased or dial-up communications line between its computer and a Reserve Bank's computer utilizing a hardware/software system certified by a Reserve Bank. The security procedure is incorporated in the hardware and software associated with the computer.[97]

The "Level Two Security Procedure" is available to any institution that issues ACH items to a Reserve Bank by electronic transmission that does not include both encryption and access controls. The procedure is also used when a bank that normally uses the Level One Security Procedure is unable to do so.

Under U.C.C. § 4A-202(c), the requirement that the security procedure be "commercially reasonable" in order for the Bank to avoid liability for an unauthorized transfer does not apply if the customer is offered a commercially reasonable security procedure but refuses the procedure and executes an agreement such as the agreement with respect to the Level Two Security Procedure in Appendix A1 of the Circular. The Federal Reserve thus implicitly states that the Level Two Security Procedure, which does not include both encryption and access controls, may not be "commercially reasonable" under U.C.C. Article 4A.

Settlement

On the settlement date, the Reserve Bank that holds the sending bank's settlement account debits or credits that account in the amount of a returned debit or credit item, and the Reserve Bank that holds the receiving bank's account credits or debits that account in the amount of the returned debit or credit item.[98]

Appendix B of Operating Circular No. 4 shows the time schedule of the Federal Reserve Bank, including the hours of the banking day, closing times, settlement dates, and standard holidays. The banking days of the Federal Reserve Bank include all days except Saturdays, Sundays, and 10 specified national holidays.

Prior to sending or receiving an item to or from a Reserve Bank, a sending bank and a receiving bank must designate to its Administration Reserve Bank (the Reserve Bank in whose District the bank is located[99]) a settlement account on a Reserve Bank's books and identify the transactions to be settled through the account.[100] A Reserve Bank may charge against the sending or receiving bank's account the amount of the bank's ACH transactions, unless the bank makes other arrangements for settlement.[101] By designating a settlement account, a bank authorizes the Reserve Bank that holds the settlement account to debit to its account on the settlement date the amount of credit items sent to the bank.

A sending or receiving bank's settlement obligation is owed to its Administrative Reserve Bank. On the settlement date,[102] the Reserve Bank that holds the sending bank's settlement account debits the account in the amount of a credit item or credits the account in the amount of a debit item. In addition, the Reserve Bank that holds the receiving bank's settlement account credits the account in the amount of a credit item or debits the account in the amount of a debit item.[103]

A Reserve Bank provides notice of credits and debits to an account holder for items for which it has agreed to settle.[104] A sending and receiving bank agree that a reasonable time to notify a Reserve Bank concerning an unauthorized or erroneously executed item is within 30 calendar days after the bank receives an advice of debit and that notice after that time may constitute the failure to exercise ordinary care, precluding the recovery of interest by the institution (with respect to a credit item subject to Article 4A) and precluding the recovery of other damages (with respect to other items).[105] The provision in the Circular implements U.C.C. § 4A-304, which allows the parties to reduce the statutory period of a reasonable time not exceeding 90 days. A sending or receiving bank is required to advise its Reserve Bank immediately if it learns of or discovers, from any source other than an advice of debit from the Reserve Bank, the possibility of error or lack of authority in the transmission or processing of an item.[106] This duty is in addition to the requirements of U.C.C. §§ 4A-204 and 4A-304, which provide for the customer's duty to notify its bank of an unauthorized or mistaken payment order advised to the customer by the bank. In both cases the penalty under U.C.C. Article 4A for noncompliance with the duty within the prescribed time period is not a shift of liability for the loss, but a loss of the sender's entitlement to interest on the amount of the loss.

"Troubled" Sending Banks

A business may find that its bank has become classified as "troubled," and this will affect the business's ACH operations. Although the business may want to change banks, that may be easier said than done, particularly if the business depends on the bank for a credit relationship.

A sending bank that has been identified by its local Reserve Bank as having financial difficulties (hereinafter a "troubled sending institution") may be required to execute the standard agreement. The agreement is designed to reduce the risk of loss or disruption by the troubled sending institution agreeing to take steps to permit its ACH credit items to be monitored and to be settled at the time of receipt by the Reserve Bank. These steps may be either notice of origination or prefunding.

A "Notice of Origination" is defined as "a written or electronic statement showing, by settlement date, the total amount of all credit items to be originated and the total amount of all debit items to be originated by the sending institution for a given ACH cycle." A Reserve Bank receiving a notice of origination may, from time to time, verify its accuracy by comparing it with the credit and debit items actually originated. It may point out discrepancies and require explanations, and where inaccurate notices are submitted, it may refuse to process ACH credit originations or to provide ACH or net settlement services.

"To prefund" is defined as "to pay, in actually and finally collected funds, to [a] Bank, the total amount of all ACH credit originations shown on a Notice of Origination prior to sending the item to this Bank for processing." Credit originations can be prefunded by a troubled sending institution by Fedwire transfer from another institution, by obtaining an advance from its Reserve Bank, or by maintaining a sufficient balance of actually and finally collected funds in its (or its correspondent's) reserve or clearing account. Unless otherwise agreed upon, the troubled sending institution authorizes the Bank, prior to processing the items, "to deduct from the sending institution's (or its correspondent's) reserve or clearing account the amount needed to prefund the ACH credits."

CROSS-BORDER PAYMENTS

The Cross-Border Council of NACHA maintains the Cross-Border Payment Operating Rules and Cross-Border Payment Operating

Guidelines. A Gateway Operator acts as the outgoing point for entries originated in the national system for transmission to another national system, and a second Gateway Operator acts as the receiving point in the other national system. The Gateway Operator that receives an entry from an ODFI within a national system for transmission abroad is the "Originating Gateway Operator" (OGO), and the Gateway Operator that receives an entry originated abroad for transmission to an RDFI within the national system is the "Receiving Gateway Operator" (RGO).

The Gateway Operator assumes responsibility for foreign exchange conversion and settlement, format mapping and translation of data, and other aspects of the cross-border funds transfer. For transactions between a U.S. financial institution and a U.S. Gateway Operator, the NACHA Operating Rules apply.

The Cross-Border Rules and Guidelines require the existence of agreements between (1) the Originator and the ODFI, (2) the ODFI and the OGO, and (3) the OGO and the RGO. The agreements must provide that the parties will be bound by the Rules and establish responsibilities, rights, and obligations in much the same manner as agreements executed in connection with the NACHA rules. ODFIs in the United States currently transmit ACH entries mostly to Canada and Mexico under the Cross-Border Rules and Guidelines and are also subject to the NACHA Rules. RDFIs in the United States that receive entries from Canada and Mexico are not subject to the Cross-Border Rules and Guidelines but are subject to the NACHA Operating Rules.

FEDERAL GOVERNMENT PAYMENTS

The federal government uses the ACH system for making payments to creditors and collecting funds from its debtors, as well as for collections from debtors. In the context of government ACH transfers, "payment applications" (credit entries) are contrasted with "collection applications" (debit entries). These can be recurring payments in the form of direct deposits to payees' accounts, such as federal salaries, Social Security payments, or veterans benefits. Credit entries for nonrecurring payments include Internal Revenue Service (IRS) tax refunds and payments to vendors under the "Vendor Express" program. The latter is a direct deposit for a business that provides goods or services to a federal agency. The format primarily used in Vendor Express is that of CCD, which facilitates a single-payment, single-addendum record (invoice).

A Pre-Authorized Debit (PAD) is currently used for ACH collections by federal agencies. A PAD is a debit entry initiated by a federal agency. A credit entry (CIE) is initiated by a debtor of a federal agency. PAD is well suited for recurring payments of a fixed or slightly varying amount, such as licensing fees, housing payments, insurance payments, overpayments, and loan repayments. Current ACH collections include delinquent taxes, funding fees on guaranteed home loans, brokerage duties, mortgage insurance premiums, and flood insurance premiums.

The setting for an ACH item initiated by a federal agency differs from the standard ACH setting in one major respect. A federal agency, as an Originator, does not use an ODFI; instead, it usually uses the Financial Management Service (FMS). The FMS is a bureau of the Department of the Treasury and serves as the U.S. government's financial manager. Besides managing federal payments and collections, the FMS is mandated to promote sound financial management practices by federal agencies, to oversee the government's central accounting and reporting system, and to provide a variety of other financial services. The FMS operates through seven financial centers throughout the United States. The originating agency delivers the items to the FMS Financial Center, usually on tapes. Payment information is then passed on to the Federal Reserve Bank in the RDFI's region.

An FMS Financial Center acts as an ODFI only insofar as communication and accounting for the Originator are concerned. The FMS is not a depository financial institution holding funds for the originating federal agency. A Federal Reserve Bank debits and credits the account of the United States Treasury for the daily ACH and checking activity, as well as for each Fedwire transfer and the clearing of government checks. Agency account-ing is carried out at the FMS. And, unless a federal government or agency has expressly agreed to be bound by the ACH Rules, the Rules do not apply to entries initiated by that entity or agency.[107]

A Reserve Bank makes the amount of all credit items sent to a receiving bank available for withdrawal or use by the receiving bank at 8:30 A.M. Eastern Time. A Reserve Bank may cease acting on a government ACH item at any time at the direction of the Treasury Department and will so notify the bank.

Pertinent Treasury regulations, together with detailed proce-dures and practices, are included in the Green Book, a proce-dural manual serving as a reference tool for all aspects of the federal government's use of the ACH system.

RISKS OF THE ACH PAYMENT SYSTEM

The ACH Rules are very specific, and the experience of financial institutions in ACH processing has, after many years, been well established. The ODFI bears the primary responsibility under the ACH Rules for the integrity of ACH transactions. The Originator, however, especially the Originator in a credit trans-fer, is bound by its contractual relationship with the ODFI and can expect that the ODFI will pass some liability to it in its ACH service agreement.

An originating business entity should focus on four areas for controlling its ACH payment system risk. The controls reflect the issues associated with computer processing of checks and elec-tronic terminal processing of outgoing wire transfers. In general, the methods of controlling electronic funds transfers should also be applied to ACH transactions.

1. The business should train its accounting and treasury personnel to have a clear understanding of the ACH Rules and any notices or reports it may receive, either as an Originator or a Receiver.

2. The business should have a daily reconciliation procedure and be prepared to notify its ODFI or RDFI of any errors or questions. The business should not neglect timely review and never miss the time deadlines of the ACH Rules. Management should review the daily procedures to be sure they are being followed properly.
3. The business should plan its continuing controls for the risks of electronic origination of entries to receive funds and the timely and accurate accounting for receipt of those funds.

   Authorizing the receipt of funds by ACH processing requires internal controls. Vendor accounts need to be so noted. Withdrawals from consumer accounts require prior written authorization.

   Electronic or manual treasury processing of ACH receipts and accounting for credit entries should be attended to, following the same criteria as for other deposits the business receives, to ensure that the correct accounts are fully credited with funds received.
4. The business should plan its continuing controls for the risks of electronic payments—controls for payment authorization and debit processing review.

Some businesses use a separate bank account for withdrawal of ACH debits, thus limiting electronic access to its funds concentration account(s)—an ACH-controlled disbursement account.

For both debit and credit ACH transactions, dollar limits can be arranged for transactions to be processed or for warning messages. For example, a business can establish a maximum dollar amount for individual ACH debits and credits, a maximum amount for a single account, or a maximum total amount for a file of ACH transactions.

A business should remember that the greatest risk in the ACH payment system is to the financial institution that originates the transaction—that is, the ODFI—and that risk is return item risk. Return item risk occurs when institutions receiving ACH debit transactions cannot, for many potential reasons, fund the transaction. Insufficient funds, stop payment orders, and unauthorized debits are the most usual reasons for return items. The ACH Rules and the time deadlines are geared to the control of return items. A business using ACH payment systems should modify its internal procedures to synchronize with its financial institution's deadlines under the ACH Rules.

ENDNOTES

1. Preface to Operating Guidelines.
2. *Id.*
3. ACH Rule 2.1.1.
4. *Id.* The agreement is not required in the case of a consumer initiated entry (CIE), and the rule does not apply to destroyed check (XCK) entries.
5. ACH Rule 2.1.2.
6. *Id.*
7. ACH Rule 1.5.
8. *Id.*
9. ACH Rule 2.1.2.
10. *Id.*
11. ACH Rule 2.1.5.
12. ACH Rules 2.8.3.10, 2.9.3.2, and 3.5.
13. ACH Rule 4.1.1. The provision does not apply to CCD credit, CTX entries, and XCK debit entries, or to MTE or SHR entries if the ODFI and RDFI are parties to a shared network agreement.
14. ACH Rule 2.1.5.
15. The notices required to be given by the ODFI to the Originator are given pursuant to § 4A-405(c) and (d) of Article 4A.
16. U.C.C. § 4A-405(d). Although U.C.C. § 4A-405(d) is not literally limited in its application to ACH transfers, Official Comment 3 to U.C.C. § 4A-405 makes clear that it was intended to apply only to ACH transfers:

A beneficiary's bank will normally accept, at the same time and as part of a single batch, payment orders with respect to many different Originators' banks. . . . The custom in ACH transactions is to release funds to the beneficiary early on the payment date even though settlement to the beneficiary's bank does not occur until later in the day. The understanding is that payments to beneficiaries are provisional until the beneficiary's bank receives settlement.

17. ACH Rule 2.2.1.1.
18. ACH Rule 2.2.1.2.
19. ACH Rule 2.2.1.3.
20. See ACH Rule 2.8 relating to the reinitiation of returned entries to originators.
21. ACH Rule 2.2.1.4.
22. ACH Rule 2.2.1.5. The warranty is not made, however, if the RDFI knows of the circumstances giving rise to the termination and the ODFI has no such knowledge.
23. ACH Rule 2.2.1.6. The warranty is not made, however, if the ODFI and the RDFI are parties to an agreement for the provision of services relating to the ACH entries or if a card issued by the ODFI to the Originator is used in connection with the authorization of these entries.
24. ACH Rule 2.2.1.7. See ACH Rule 4.5 with respect to the provision of periodic statements.
25. See ACH Rules 2.6 and 4.7.
26. ACH Rule 2.2.1.8. The warranties are also made in connection with written demands for payment transmitted to the RDFI outside the ACH system.
27. ACH Rule 2.2.1.9. Under ACH Rule 2.2.4, the ODFI warranties under the ACH Rules are also made to sending points.
28. ACH Rule 2.2.3 applies to the liability of the ODFI in the event that the ODFI is in breach of any of its warranties.
29. ACH Rule 2.2.2.

30. ACH Rule 2.3.1.
31. ACH Rule 2.3.2.
32. *Id.*
33. See ACH Rule 5.3.
34. ACH Rule 2.4.1.
35. ACH Rule 2.4.2. It should be noted that ACH Rule 1.3 (with respect to a participating depository financial institution) and ACH Rule 8.5 (with respect to an ACH Operator) allow participating depository financial institutions and ACH Operators to extend deadlines in circumstances beyond their control if diligence has been exercised.
36. ACH Rule 13.1.41.
37. ACH Rule 2.4.4.
38. ACH Rule 2.4.2.
39. ACH Rule 2.4.3.
40. ACH Rule 2.4.5.
41. See Geva, *The Law of Electronic Funds Transfers,* 85.05[4][d].
42. ACH Rule 2.5.1.
43. ACH Rule 13.1.41.
44. ACH Rule 2.4.2.
45. ACH Rule 2.4.5.
46. ACH Rule 2.7.1.
47. ACH Rule 2.7.2.
48. ACH Rule 2.2.
49. ACH Rule 2.7.3.
50. ACH Rule 5.1.
51. ACH Rule 2.7.6.
52. ACH Rule 2.11. Separate reinitiation rules apply to RCK entries.
53. ACH Rule 2.1.2.
54. The RDFI has the right to request the authorization under ACH Rule 4.1.1. Under ACH Rule 3.5, the Originator's record keeping obligation does not apply to shared network or machine terminal entries if the ODFI and RDFI are parties to an agreement for the provision of services relating to the entries.

55. ACH Rule 3.2. The rule does not apply to SHR or MTE entries if the ODFI and RDFI are parties to an agreement for the provision of services relating to such entries or if a card issued by the ODFFI or the Originator is used in connection with the authorization of the entries.
56. ACH Rule 3.3.1.
57. ACH Rule 3.3.2.
58. ACH Rule 3.3.3.
59. ACH Rule 3.3.4. The parallel rule in Regulation E is § 205.10(b), which requires the person who obtains the consumer's authorization to provide a copy to the consumer.
60. ACH Rule 4.1.1.
61. *Id.* The Rule does not apply to SHR or MTE when the ODFI and the RDFI are parties to an agreement for the provision of services relating to the entries.
62. ACH Rule 4.1.2.
63. ACH Rule 4.1.3. The Rule obligates the RDFI to accept other entries as well, but subject to its right to return or reject entries. The RDFI has a broad right to return entries under Rule 5.1.
64. ACH Rule 4.1.4. See Chapter 5 for the similar rule relating to beneficiaries' names and numbers under Article 4A.
65. ACH Rule 4.2.
66. ACH Rule 4.4.1.
67. An entry is "received" on the banking day that it is made available to the RDFI. The entry is made "available" to the RDFI or its receiving point when it has been processed by the RDFI's ACH Operator and is ready for distribution. ACH Rule 4.3.
68. ACH Rule 4.4.1.
69. ACH Rule 4.4.7.
70. ACH Rule 4.4.2.
71. ACH Rule 13.1.41. The date on which the Originator expects payment to occur is the "effective entry date." The ACH Operator establishes the settlement date by reading the effective entry date. The settlement date is either the

effective entry date or the next available business date. See "effective entry date" in the Glossary to the ACH Rules.

72. ACH Rule 4.4.3.

73. ACH Rule 4.6.

74. ACH Rule 4.5.

75. ACH Rule 4.4.5.

76. U.C.C. § 4-401(a). See Geva, *The Law of Electronic Funds Transfers*, Appendix G, for a list of Article 4A provisions that might apply to ACH debit transfers. An RCK entry is treated as an Article 4 item only for purposes of the Article 4 presentment and notice of dishonor rules.

77. U.C.C. § 3-406.

78. See Chapter 3.

79. ACH Rule 4.4.4. The Rule does not apply to machine terminal (MTE), point-of-sale (POS), preauthorized payments and deposits (PPD), or shared network (SHR) entries.

80. ACH Rule 1.3. Of course, the rule that an action to be taken on a day that is not a banking day is excused until the next banking day, under ACH Rule 1.4, would also apply.

81. ACH Rule 5.2.1.

82. *Id.*

83. ACH Rule 5.2.2.

84. *Id.*

85. ACH Rule 5.2.3.

86. ACH Rule 5.3.2.

87. ACH Rule 5.5. "Second banking day" refers to the second banking day of the RDFI's ACH Operator.

88. The Circular's appendixes provide a description of the security procedures (Appendix A), an agreement relating to the security procedures (Appendix A-1), a time schedule for ACH items (Appendix B), a prefunding agreement for an institution in financial difficulties (Appendix C), forms by which a sending institution (Appendix C-1) or a sending institution and its correspondent (Appendix C-2) consent to the Agreement in Appendix C, and a statement

describing the Reserve Bank's handling of federal government ACH items (Appendix D).

89. Operating Circular No. 4, § 1.0.

90. Operating Circular No. 4, § 1.3. The version adopted is the version contained in Appendix B of Regulation J, including provisions of Article 1 referred to in Article 4A, as may be approved from time to time by the U.C.C. sponsors, the National Conference of Commissioners on Uniform State Laws, and the American Law Institute. Operating Circular No. 4, § 1.0.

91. Operating Circular No. 4, § 2.1(e).

92. 894 F. Supp. 1470 (1995).

93. Under U.C.C. 4-301, a payor bank may return an item before it has made final payment and before its midnight deadline.

94. ACH Rule 5.1.2.

95. Operating Circular No. 4, § 4.1.

96. *Id.*

97. Operating Circular No. 4, Appendix A, § 2.

98. Operating Circular No. 4, § 14.2.

99. Operating Circular No. 4, § 2.1(c).

100. Operating Circular No. 4, § 9.1.

101. Operating Circular No. 4, § 9.2.

102. "Settlement date" is defined in § 2.1(t) of the Circular as the date for settlement of an item as provided in the Circular.

103. Operating Circular No. 4, § 10.2.

104. Operating Circular No. 4, § 16.1.

105. Operating Circular No. 4, § 16.2.

106. Operating Circular No. 4, § 16.3.

107. ACH Rule 1.1.

7

Commerce and Payments in Cyberspace

Electronics and the Internet have created great changes in how commerce is conducted and payments are made in the United States. This chapter considers how communications can legally bind the parties despite the absence of a signed, written agreement. It discusses "digital signatures"; "electronic checks," bill payment and presentment; procurement; "smart cards," including purchasing cards and stored value cards; home banking; money laundering; and the privacy rights of bank customers.

REVOLUTIONS IN PAYMENT SYSTEMS

The last half of the twentieth century and the beginning of the twenty-first century witnessed revolutionary developments in payment systems in the United States.

Checks today are processed with magnetic ink character recognition (MICR) line coding near the bottom of the check, a technology that was developed in the 1950s. The 1970s saw the advent of the fax machine, the automated teller machine (ATM),

185

the point-of-sale (POS) machine, and the processing of checks through automated clearing house (ACH) associations. In the 1960s and 1970s, the Federal Reserve Wire Network (Fedwire), the New York Clearing House Association's Clearing House Interbank Payments System (CHIPS), and the Society for Worldwide Interbank Funds Transfers (SWIFT) were created and became important means of sending large-dollar wire transfers on an automated basis, both domestically and internationally. The 1980s saw the development of the personal computer (PC).

The 1990s saw the mushrooming of applications for the computer and the popularization of e-mail, browsing on the World Wide Web, electronic commerce transacted on the Internet, and the proliferation of new electronic payment products. Payment system law has sometimes struggled to keep pace with these developments but, on the whole, has managed rather well.

PAPERLESS TRANSACTIONS AND COMMUNICATIONS

Consider three types of transactions: In the first transaction, a consumer wants to buy this book. The consumer goes on-line to the Internet, points the browser to an e-commerce bookseller, and orders the book. On the web site, the consumer is asked to provide a credit card number. The consumer gives the number and clicks on the appropriate box or icon to confirm the order. The web site uses an attribution procedure to verify the confidentiality and integrity of the consumer's message. A chain of messages from the web site to the bank that issued the credit card, and to the merchant's bank, results in the payment to the merchant. The charge to the consumer appears on the consumer's next monthly statement from the credit card issuer. The transaction is traditionally finalized, from the consumer's point of view, when the consumer's check to the credit card issuer is paid by the consumer's bank. In today's environment, the consumer may alternatively pay the credit card issuer via the Internet, by visiting the issuer's web site, or by utilizing the services of a consolidator that provides electronic bill presentment and payment services.

In the second transaction, an investment company wishes to purchase stock for $50,000 through a stock brokerage firm. The company sends an order to the brokerage firm by e-mail, using an encryption method that the parties have agreed to use for security purposes. The brokerage firm decrypts the message, acknowledges receipt of the order by encrypted e-mail to the investment company, and purchases the stock for the account of the company. There is no signed customer agreement between the company and the brokerage firm.

In the third transaction, a large automobile manufacturing company purchases parts and supplies from a supply company. A computer at the manufacturer's plant monitors the level of parts and supplies maintained by the manufacturer. When the supply on hand of a part required in the manufacture of a carburetor drops below the desired level, the computer automatically orders an additional supply of the part from the supply company by e-mail, using an encryption method. A computer at the supply company decrypts the message, acknowledges receipt of the message by e-mail to the manufacturer, instructs the shipping department to send the parts to the manufacturer, and bills the manufacturer for the parts. The computer at the manufacturer's office sends a wire transfer to the supply company's bank, referencing the invoice number and providing other information relating to the sales transaction. In this transaction, the parts are ordered and paid for essentially on a wholly automated basis.

The transactions described here are examples of electronic commerce on the Internet. Although any of the documents generated in the parties' computers can be printed out, the documentation consists of electronic records, not paper records, and the process of contracting between the parties is a wholly electronic and paperless process.

Statute of Frauds

All 50 states have enacted laws that generally require contractual undertakings to be in writing and signed by the parties obligated to perform under the contract. These laws are known as the "statute of frauds."

The term *statute of frauds* is probably inapt. The statutes do not directly address liability for fraud; rather, their purpose is to eliminate litigation over oral obligations. If the party claiming the right to payment, for example, is unable to produce a written document in which the other party has agreed to make the payment, then the claimant cannot enforce the alleged payment obligation in court. A great deal of difficult litigation that might otherwise clog the courts is thereby eliminated.

The statute of frauds typically applies to obligations that exceed a minimum amount. For example, suppose that the statute of frauds applicable to the transactions in the examples given here provides that any obligation in excess of $500 must be stated in a written document. Suppose also that the buyer of this book repudiates its obligation to buy the book on the grounds that there was no agreement in writing signed by the buyer to buy the book. The statute of frauds will not support the buyer's position, because the purchase price of the book is less than $500 and the statute of frauds does not apply to obligations of less than $500.

If the company that ordered stock through a brokerage firm repudiates its obligation to purchase the stock, the statute of frauds will support the company's position, because the purchase price for the stock is $50,000, that is, in excess of the $500 statute of frauds amount. The brokerage firm cannot enforce the buyer's obligation, because the company did not execute an agreement in writing to buy the stock.

Uniform Electronic Transactions Act and Electronic Signatures in Global and National Commerce Act

To facilitate electronic commerce, many states have adopted a law known as the Uniform Electronic Transactions Act (UETA) and Congress has enacted the Electronic Signatures in Global and National Commerce Act (E-SIGN). E-SIGN was enacted by

Congress generally subsequent to the adoption of the UETA by the states that have adopted it. Generally, E-SIGN, as the federal law, preempts the UETA, but a provision of E-SIGN states that the UETA, rather than E-SIGN, will prevail in a state that has adopted the UETA in substantially the same form as the UETA proposed by the uniform law commissioners who drafted it.

The UETA and E-SIGN apply to "records," which consist of information inscribed on a tangible medium or stored in an electronic or other medium and are retrievable in perceivable form. Thus, a message stored in a computer's hard drive that is "perceivable" by viewing on a monitor, or by printing the message, is a record.

The most significant of the provisions of E-SIGN and the UETA states simply that contractual obligations need not be in writing but may instead be documented as an electronic record. Electronic records are placed on an equal footing with paper records. This provision applies despite the existence of a statute of frauds that would otherwise deny the legal effect or validity of the paperless electronic record.

Traditional contract law requires that a party cannot be forced to perform a contractual obligation unless that party has *signed* the contract. E-SIGN and the UETA place an "electronic signature" on an equal footing with a handwritten signature. A person's name typed on a computer keyboard might constitute an identifying symbol, adopted by the person typing the name, as part of the electronic record in which the name is typed. If the sender of an electronic record encrypts the record so that the receiving party must decrypt it in order to understand it, the sender has "signed" the record by encrypting it. The typed name constitutes an "electronic signature" and is binding as a signature under the UETA and E-SIGN.

PUBLIC KEY INFRASTRUCTURE

Digital Signatures

An "electronic signature" and a "digital signature" are not the same; these terms have quite different meanings as they are generally used today. An electronic signature, under E-SIGN and the UETA, is, broadly, a symbol or process used for purposes of identification that is adopted as part of a record. Such a process would include the encryption of a record. The term *digital signature*, however, is commonly used to refer more narrowly to the encryption of a record as part of a cryptographic process that includes what are known as "private keys" and "public keys." Thus, the term *electronic signature* generally includes a digital signature, as utilized in the public key infrastructure discussed below.

Private Keys

The two parties in a private key transaction share the same code to encrypt and decrypt a message. Because the same key is used for encryption and decryption, this cryptography is called "symmetric" cryptography. The "Captain Midnight" code is an example of a symmetric private key. In that code, "A" equals "Z," "B" equals "Y," and so on. "Captain Midnight" is "Xzkgzrm Nrwmrtsg." Captain Midnight refers to the radio show hero's secret code.

Private key cryptography works very well in closed systems with a limited number of participants. The private key concept, however, is subject to question in an open system, like the Internet, because no distribution method can securely deliver all the keys to everyone needing a digital signature on the Internet. In particular, persons who have never communicated with each other cannot both have knowledge of the key.

Public Keys

The problem of private key distribution is solved in the "public key infrastructure" (PKI) with two keys. The owner has both a private key and a public key. The private key, of course, is maintained with great secrecy, but the public key of the owner is widely distributed, often even available through the Internet. The public and private keys are related mathematically, but it is not computationally feasible to derive one key on the basis of knowledge of the other.

In the public key infrastructure, the sender of an electronic message creates a "message digest" and encrypts the digest, utilizing the private key of the sender. The encrypted digest is the "digital signature." The recipient of the message then uses the public key of the sender to decrypt the message.

Certifying Authorities

One problem remains in the public key infrastructure: How can the receiver have confidence that the key obtained publicly is in actual fact the authentic key of the sender?

The public key infrastructure seeks to solve this problem by using a trusted third party as a certifying authority (CA), which may be a bank or a bank consortium. The CA issues certificates to its subscribers. A certificate issued by the CA identifies the CA, identifies the subscriber, contains the subscriber's public key, states the time period in which the public key is operational, and is digitally signed by the CA.

The subscriber sends the certificate to persons with whom the subscriber wishes to do business, and those persons rely on the certificate as proof of the subscriber's identity. Because the certificate is digitally signed (see the earlier description of digital signatures) by the CA, the recipient of the certificate can use the public key of the CA to verify the digital signature of the CA on the certificate.

ELECTRONIC CHECKS

The term *electronic check* (or *e-check*) refers rather vaguely to paperless payment systems. More specifically, the term may be applied to the conversion of a consumer's check into an ACH debit transfer, as described in the discussion of ACH transactions in Chapter 6. It may also be applied to telephone-initiated or Internet-initiated ACH transactions.

Check conversion at the point of purchase is a good illustration of what may be called an "electronic check" transaction. For example, the consumer at a department store hands a check to the clerk at the cash register. The merchant inserts the check into a check reader that records the routing number, account number, and check number from the MICR line on the check. A sign may be posted next to the cash register indicating that checks presented at the register may be used to create "electronic checks" to be sent for collection by debits to the consumer's account. The cashier voids the check and gives the consumer the voided check and a receipt. The monthly bank statement received by the consumer shows the merchant's name as well as the check number and the date of the debit.

The great advantage of check conversion for merchants is in the cost savings—in particular, savings in front-end and back-office time and labor in collecting and reconciling checks for deposit into the merchant's depository bank, as well as in check deposit and encoding fees. In addition, the merchant receives earlier notification of returned checks, approximately 3 to 6 days in the case of a returned ACH debit entry, as opposed to about 8 to 12 days for a paper check. The earlier notice improves collection efforts and fraud detection.

Other examples of ACH transactions that can be described as involving electronic checks are "accounts receivable" entries, "returned check" entries, "telephone-initiated" entries, and "Internet-initiated" entries.

An accounts receivable entry and a returned check entry also start with a consumer's check. In an accounts receivable entry, the consumer mails the check to a merchant or to the merchant's dropbox. Instead of depositing the check, the merchant voids it and uses the information on the check to initiate a debit entry to the consumer's account. In a returned check entry, the merchant uses the information on a check that has been returned for insufficient funds to initiate the debit entry to the consumer's account.

In a telephone-initiated entry, the consumer authorizes a merchant over the telephone to initiate the debit transfer. The ACH rules allow such entries only if the consumer has purchased goods from the merchant within the past two years, there is a written agreement between the consumer and the merchant, or it is the consumer (not the merchant) who initiated the telephone call. In an Internet-initiated entry, the consumer authorizes a merchant to initiate a debit transfer from the consumer's account while the consumer is shopping on the merchant's web site.

ELECTRONIC BILL PRESENTMENT AND PAYMENT

In the electronic bill presentment and payment (EBPP) environment, three business models are used:

1. *Biller-Direct Model.* The bill payor goes on-line to the biller's web site to retrieve and pay on-line the biller's bills.
2. *Customer Consolidation Model.* Each biller goes on-line to a specified web site and posts its bills, including the payment information. Then a customer goes to the site to review and pay the bills posted by the various billers.
3. *Service Provider Consolidator Model.* A consolidator consolidates the bills of multiple billers for access by the payers at the service provider's web site. In the service provider consolidator model, the service provider consolidator typically displays a summary of each bill (the "thin" model in EBPP parlance). If the payer wants complete detailed billing information (the "thick" model), a link to the biller's web site normally offers the means to satisfy the payor's needs.

B2B versus B2C

In EBPP, a distinction is made between systems for consumer payments and those for business payments. Business-to-business systems are known as B2B ("be-to-be") and business-to-consumer systems as B2C ("be-to-see").

EBPP Advantages for Business Billers. In the more sophisticated EBPP systems, when a bill has been paid, the system allows the biller to credit the payment to the payor's account receivable.

Another advantage to the billers that use an EBPP system is the elimination of the costly paperwork of printing, stuffing, and mailing bills. Also eliminated is the processing of customers' checks, which includes a reduction of bank charges (e.g., for check deposit, check encoding, and lockbox processing).

ELECTRONIC PROCUREMENT

Many organizations address procurement, purchasing, and payments as three separate paper-based processes. For any one item, a company researches products and suppliers, submits a purchase order, and buys the product. The process can take days or weeks, with associated personnel expense. Using the Internet can reduce the purchasing and procurement cycle to a few days or hours and reduce transaction costs as well.

Smart Cards

A **smart card** is a card about the size of a credit card that contains an integrated microcomputer chip. The card has the capacity to store different types of information, including account numbers and credit lines and other data that can allow it to be used as both a credit card and a debit card, that is a card that can create debits to the bank account of a consumer, the employer of the card holder, or a trading partner. In addition, the smart card may hold personal information, such as health data, and may be used as a security token for the prevention of fraud. Smart cards may be used as purchasing cards or as stored value cards, but not all such cards have the capacity to debit a bank account.

Purchasing Cards

The most common form of purchasing card is used for the recording and control of the travel and entertainment (T&E) expenses of a company's employees. These cards greatly simplify the process of filling out travel and expense forms and help to reconcile expense reports, allocate expenses by category, create travel and expense reports, and provide data to the card users and company managers via the Internet or through corporate intranets. The T&E cards can greatly reduce the cost of processing expense reports and speed up reimbursement to the employee.

A more ambitious form of purchasing card combines T&E reporting with general procurement. For example, a company may use a purchasing card that automatically reconciles and integrates a charge to the card for supplies and inventory into the general ledger of the company. That use can result in considerable savings in the costs of buying, paying, and reconciliation.

A significant advantage of the use of a purchase card as part of an electronic procurement system is the ability of the card to authenticate the originator. In effect, the use of the card automatically transmits to the recipient of any communication the "digital signature" of the sender.

Stored Value Cards

Stored value cards may be either smart cards or cards that use magnetic stripe technology. Stored value cards have been in use in Europe for a number of years and are widely accepted there. They have not been as widely accepted in the United States.

A **stored value card** typically allows a consumer to place "value" on the card and to download that value at the place where payment is to be made. For example, value may be placed on a card at an ATM or at the counter of the bank. The consumer may then present the card at the cash register of a merchant, and the cashier inserts the card into a terminal that will download the value from the card for credit to the merchant's account.

Closed System Stored Value Card. A stored value card that is used in a closed system is limited in how it may be used. Prepaid telephone cards, for example, that are used to pay for telephone calls operate in a closed system, because they can be used only for that purpose and only through the telephone company or companies that are a part of the system. For example, the card issued by the New York City Metropolitan Transit Authority (MTA) may be used only to pay the MTA for bus and subway transportation in that city.

A card that is used in a closed system may, however, be used within that system for many purposes. At the Marine Corps training camp at Camp Lejeune, North Carolina, for example, stored value cards issued to the Marines are used to pay for haircuts, soft drinks, and bowling games and to check out assault weapons from the armory. A card issued by a university is typically used in that university's closed system, but it may be used within the system for a variety of purposes, such as to pay for books, food, transportation, lodging, photocopying, and other services.

A relatively recent type of stored value card is the payroll payment card. A payment card can be issued to an employee in lieu of a payroll check. Especially in a case in which direct deposit by ACH transfer to the employee's account is not feasible—the situation for an employee who has no bank account—a payment card may be a useful alternative.

A payment card can be issued with the value already stored on the card or issued in a form that will allow the employee to load value onto the card at the counter of a bank or at an ATM machine. Some payment cards can be used, as conventional stored value cards are used, to download value at the terminal of a merchant in order to pay for purchased consumer goods.

Open System Stored Value Card. An example of an open system is the joint Visa and MasterCard pilot program conducted in late 1997 on the Upper West Side of New York City. Free cards were offered and some terminals were given free to merchants, but the results were disappointing and the program terminated in 1998.

Home Banking. A bank customer may use a personal computer to pay merchants for personal, family, or household expenses. Home banking allows the customer to view account balances, review recent transactions, transfer funds between accounts at the bank, order documents, establish automatic transfers (such as the direct deposit of paychecks and the automatic payment of insurance premiums), and communicate with the bank via e-mail.

The one feature that is not yet available to the consumer sitting at the computer is the delivery of cash in the form of deposits to and withdrawals from the bank. Perhaps at some time in the future stored value cards can be used to allow the consumer to transfer value from an account at the bank to the card at home in much the same way in which value is transferred from an account to a stored value card at an ATM.

MONEY LAUNDERING

Money laundering is a process by which funds obtained illegally are made to appear to have been obtained legally. Money laundering is typically difficult to detect and may be even more difficult to detect when the wrongdoer uses electronic funds transfers.

The principal legislation applicable to money laundering in the United States is the Bank Secrecy Act. The Act and its regulations make money laundering illegal and require covered institutions to disclose certain transactions. The Financial Crimes Enforcement Network (FinCEN) of the Treasury Department has primary responsibility for enforcing the Act.

The USA Patriot Act, enacted in 2001, adopted new provisions and amended the Bank Secrecy Act to broaden its anti-money laundering provisions, make certain records accessible to federal authorities, and require covered institutions to take special measures and exercise special diligence with respect to accounts maintained for non-U.S. persons.

The institutions are required to file Currency Transaction Reports (CTRs) with respect to large currency transactions and Suspicious Activity Reports (SARs) with respect to transactions that appear to indicate money laundering or other suspicious conduct. A CTR is required for a transaction of $10,000 or more.

A suspicious transaction must be reported if it involved $5,000 or more in funds or other assets and the bank or broker dealer has reason to suspect that the funds were diverted from illegal activities or the transaction is intended to hide illegal funds sources. A transaction is also suspicious when it involves the layering of a series of transactions broken down into amounts of less than $10,000 to avoid the filing of a CTR or if it has no business or apparent lawful purpose or is not the sort in which the customer would normally be expected to engage and the firm knows of no reasonable explanation for the transaction after examining the available facts.

Just as FinCEN is the money laundering watchdog in the United States, the Financial Action Task Force (FATF) is the international watchdog. The FATF was created by the Group of Seven Nations for the purpose of developing and promoting programs to deter money laundering. The FATF publishes an annual report on money laundering activities and has issued "40 Recommendations" as part of its mission to deter money laundering.

In addition to banks, there are many nondepository money-service businesses (MSBs) that provide financial services, such as money transmitters, check cashers, and foreign currency exchanges. The MSBs generally receive less attention by regulators than do the banks. A number of states have adopted legislation that attempts to address the activities of MSBs, but the lack of effective oversight has made meaningful enforcement difficult.

PRIVACY RIGHTS

An important issue in the detection of money laundering is concern for the privacy rights of the customers of the banks. The Gramm-Leach-Bliley Act restricts the ability of a bank or other financial institution to disclose nonpublic, personal information about a consumer to nonaffiliated third parties. The Act also requires the institutions to disclose to their customers their privacy policies and practices as they relate to the sharing of information with both affiliates and nonaffiliated third parties.

The Federal Reserve has adopted regulations for the purpose of implementing the Act. The Federal Reserve regulations generally require a financial institution to make an initial disclosure, and then periodically an annual disclosure, to its customers that describes the institution's privacy policies. The Act and the regulations thus deal with two kinds of disclosures. First, the financial institution is prohibited from disclosing private information about its customers. Second, the Act requires that the institution disclose to its customers information about its privacy policies.

Unless an exception applies or the customer has "opted out" of the requirements of the Act, the Act prohibits an institution from disclosing "nonpublic" information to a nonaffiliated third party. The Act also prohibits such disclosure if the institution has not made the disclosures to the customer that the Act requires the institution to make.

The disclosures required by the Act must inform the customer that the institution does not disclose nonpublic personal information about its current and former customers to affiliates or nonaffiliated third parties, except as authorized by the Act. The disclosures must also describe the categories of nonpublic personal information collected by the institution and the institution's policies and practices with respect to protecting the confidentiality and security of nonpublic personal information.

An institution may not claim that a customer has opted out of the privacy provisions of the Act unless:

- The bank has provided an "opt out'" notice to the consumer,
- The bank has given the consumer a reasonable opportunity, before it discloses the information, to opt out of the disclosure, and
- The consumer has not, in fact, opted out.

As noted earlier, the privacy provisions relate to the bank's disclosing "nonpublic" information. There is no restriction on the disclosure of information that is "public" information. Nonpublic information includes personally identifiable financial information as well as lists or description of consumers that are derived by the use of personally identifiable financial information.

INTEGRATING RISK MANAGEMENT

Risk management of commerce and payments in cyberspace should be integrated into a company's risk management plan and monitoring of its corporate payment systems. These innovations should not be regarded as more secure because they are new and technologically impressive.

8

Management of Corporate Payment Systems Risks

This chapter discusses risk management for corporate payment systems risks. Suggestions for treasury operations and internal controls, a review of how risks are allocated in the company's agreement with its banks, and a typical crime policy insurance checklist are included.

RISK MANAGEMENT

Risk management is a planned and systematic process designed to eliminate, or at least to reduce, the probability that losses will occur. Risk management concepts and procedures should guide corporate policy. Meeting the reasonable expectations of the insurers should help to control premium costs and maximize coverage benefits, as well as to reduce the likelihood of the occurrence of the covered event.

The goal of managing corporate payment systems risks is to ensure that the company maintains control of its obligation to make and its right to receive payments. The consequences of failure can be great. Some companies have lost huge amounts, and some have become bankrupt because of their failure to control liquidity or because of losses resulting from fraud.

Transaction Risk

The Office of the Controller of the Currency (OCC), in OCC Bulletin 98-3, summarizes transaction risk, in part:

> *Transaction risk* is associated with internal controls, data integrity, transaction rules, employee performance and operating procedures or problems with service or delivery because of design deficiencies. Transaction risk has the potential to adversely impact earnings and capital as a result of fraud, error, and the inability to deliver products or services, maintain a competitive position and manage information. Transaction risk is evident in every product and service offered.

The risks of corporate payment systems are primarily and best managed by avoidance of risks—preventing losses in the payment systems of both funds due to and due from the corporation. Loss prevention measures will mitigate or prevent a loss. Usually, the cost of loss prevention is far less than the funds that would otherwise be lost; even an insured loss typically has a deductible and can result in an increased premium.

Good internal controls should protect every honest employee.

The process of creating checklists will help identify activities and situations that may give rise to events or incidents of potential loss for the corporation, its employees, and its suppliers or vendors. Creating a checklist is a good way to develop comprehensive written procedures with an easily accessible table of contents and index.

Exhibit 8.1 is an insurance policy application and checklist for crime coverage. The checklist provides a basis for any corporate checklist involving executive, managerial, and clerical controls for corporate payment systems risk management.

Exhibit 8.1 Risk Management—Crime Coverage Checklist and Application

General Information:

Name of Applicant: _____

Principal Address: _____

Date Business Established: _____

Present Crime Insurance Program:

    a) Insurance Carrier: _____

    b) Limit of Liability: _____

    c) Effective Date: _____

Description of Business Operations: _____

_____

_____

In the course of your business, do you perform any of the following functions?

    a) Trading: ❏ Yes ❏ No

    b) Extending Credit: ❏ Yes ❏ No

    c) Issuing Warehouse Receipts: ❏ Yes ❏ No

    d) Transporting or Storing Valuables for Others: ❏ Yes ❏ No

    e) Leasing: ❏ Yes ❏ No

Number of Employees:

    a) Foreign _____

    b) Domestic _____

    c) With Access to Money or Securities _____

Do you have established procedures for recruiting staff and assessing their suitability for positions of trust?

    ❏ Yes ❏ No

Number of Locations:

    a) Foreign _____

    b) Domestic _____

Proposed Effective Date of Coverage: _____

Coverage Requested:

Insuring Clause:	Limit of Liability	Deductible(s)
A. Employee Theft	$_____	$_____
B. Forgery, Alteration, and Counterfeiting	$_____	$_____
C. Theft, Disappearance, and Destruction	$_____	$_____
D. Computer and Funds Transfer Fraud	$_____	$_____
E. Audit Expense (up to $ ____,000)	$_____	$_____

Coverage Extensions:

1. If coverage is required on your appointed or elected agents, whether they be persons, partnerships, limited liability companies, or corporations performing any act or service in connection with the ordinary conduct of your business, complete the following for each:

    Name and Location   Amount of Coverage

2. If coverage is required on your partners, complete the following:

    Name and Location   Amount of Coverage

(Continues)

Management of Corporate Payment Systems Risks

Exhibit 8.1 Continued

3. If excess employee dishonesty coverage for specified employees is desired, complete the following:

	Name Schedule Coverage		Position Schedule Coverage	
Excess Limit on Each	Name of Employee	Position Title	# of Employees	Location

Internal Controls / Audit Procedures:

External Audits:

1. Does an independent CPA audit your books at least annually? ❑ Yes ❑ No
   a) If "Yes," by whom? _____
   b) If "No," please attach an explanation.
2. Does the audit include a review of EDP Department? ❑ Yes ❑ No
3. Are the audits complete and unqualified? ❑ Yes ❑ No (If "No," please attach an explanation.)
4. Are all locations and entities audited? ❑ Yes ❑ No (If "No," please attach description of the extent of your audit.)
5. Have you changed CPAs in the past three (3) years? ❑ Yes ❑ No (If "Yes," please attach an explanation.)
6. Have they made any recommendations about internal systems that have not been implemented? ❑ Yes ❑ No (If "Yes," please attach an explanation.)
7. Does the CPA provide a Management Letter? ❑ Yes ❑ No (If "Yes," please include the most recent copy and applicant's response to the letter.)

Internal Audit:

1. Is there an Internal Audit Department responsible for the oversight and review of internal audit programs for all business operations — including the EDP Department? ❑ Yes ❑ No (If "No," please attach an explanation of how this function is fulfilled.)
2. How many people are employed in the Internal Audit Department? _____
3. To whom does the Internal Audit Department report? _____
4. How often are full internal audits made of all locations? _____
5. Do they carry out regular, random, unscheduled checks on stocks or raw materials, work in progress, and finished goods? ❑ Yes ❑ No

Controls:

1. Do the employees who reconcile monthly bank statements also:
   a) Sign checks? ❑ Yes ❑ No
   b) Handle deposits? ❑ Yes ❑ No
   c) Have access to check-signing machines or signature plates? ❑ Yes ❑ No

NOTE: If answer to any of the above is "Yes," please attach explanation of the other controls that are in place for these procedures.

2. Is countersignature required on checks issued by the applicant? ❑ Yes ❑ No (If "No," please attach an explanation of procedures employed.)
3. Do all requisitions and purchase orders require the prior approval of authorized personnel? ❑ Yes ❑ No (If "No," please attach an explanation of procedure(s) followed.)
4. Are supplier's invoices matched with related purchase orders, receiving reports, and authorized vendor lists for review prior to each cash disbursement? ❑ Yes ❑ No (If "No," please attach a description of procedures followed.)

Exhibit 8.1   Continued

5. Is a complete inventory made, with a physical check of stock and equipment? ❑ Yes ❑ No
    a) Do you handle any securities?   ❑ Yes ❑ No
    b) If "Yes," what is the value of securities held? _____

6. Are securities subject to joint control of two or more authorized employees? ❑ Yes ❑ No

7. Are monthly statements of account sent to customers independently of employees receiving payment?
                                                                                  ❑ Yes   ❑ No

8. Are invoices stamped "paid" at the time checks are issued to prevent duplicate checks from being
    issued to fictitious persons?   ❑ Yes ❑ No

9. Are duties of employees segregated so that no individual can control any of the following transactions
    from commencement to completion:

    a. Signing of checks above US $50,000?   ❑ Yes   ❑ No
    b. Issuing funds transfer instructions?   ❑ Yes   ❑ No
    c. Issuing amendments to funds transfer procedures?   ❑ Yes   ❑ No
    d. Investments in and custody of securities or other values (including blank checks,
        travelers checks, bills of exchange, etc.)?   ❑ Yes   ❑ No
    e. Authorized capital expenditures?   ❑ Yes   ❑ No
            Please advise details of the levels of authority for capital expenditures within your
            business unit.

Officer	Authority Limit ($ MM)
CEO	
CFO	
Others	

10. Are passwords used to afford varying levels of entry to the computer system, and are they regularly
    changed when there is any turnover in knowledgeable personnel?
                                                                                  ❑ Yes ❑ No

11. Is there any precious metal or gem exposure (gold, silver, platinum, industrial diamonds, etc.)?
                                                                                  ❑ Yes ❑ No
    a. If "Yes," what is the approximate value of these items? _____

Funds Transfer:

1. What is the total annual value of all funds transfers? _____

2. What is the average value of a transfer? _____

3. Are there specific arrangements with banks as to the individuals in your Company authorized to:

    a) Transfer funds?   ❑ Yes ❑ No
    b) Request changes in procedures?   ❑ Yes ❑ No
    c) Obtain records?   ❑ Yes ❑ No
    *Please attach a description of the internal controls that ensure that fraudulent instructions
    cannot be given to any bank by persons either with or without authority to give genuine
    instructions.*

4. Are all banks required to authenticate any funds-transfer instructions before payment? ❑ Yes ❑ No
    (If "Yes," how is this achieved?)_____
    _____

(Continues)

Exhibit 8.1 Continued

5. Are all banks required to confirm funds-transfer transactions in writing within 24 hours? ❏ Yes ❏ No

6. Are all funds-transfer instructions given to financial institutions on a preformatted basis? ❏ Yes ❏ No

7. Are there independent checks of funds-transfer records by staff not authorized to handle/instruct such transfers? ❏ Yes ❏ No

Other:

1. What is the maximum amount of the following kept on premises:
   - a. Cash? $ _____
   - b. Checks? $ _____
   - c. Securities? $ _____

Total:

2. Is the above kept in a safe or vault? ❏ Yes ❏ No (If "No," please describe where kept.)

3. Are any of the following types of alarms on premises?
   - a. Location # _____ ❏ Holdup ❏ Burglary ❏ Central Station
     ❏ Local Gong Devices ❏ Police Connection ❏ Ultrasonic
   - b. Location # _____ ❏ Holdup ❏ Burglary ❏ Central Station
     ❏ Local Gong Devices ❏ Police Connection ❏ Ultrasonic

4. Are money, securities, etc. transported to the bank:
   - d. Every day? ❏ Yes ❏ No
   - e. Whenever a specified $ threshold is reached? ❏ Yes ❏ No

5. Maximum amount carried by messengers? $ _____

6. Do messengers vary the time of day at which they go to the bank? ❏ Yes ❏ No

7. Does a guard accompany messengers? ❏ Yes ❏ No

8. Is the guard armed? ❏ Yes ❏ No

9. Do messengers use locked satchels? ❏ Yes ❏ No

8. Do messengers, salespersons, or any other employees keep money or other valuables at home at night or on weekends? ❏ Yes ❏ No
   (If "Yes," please attach an explanation, including the approximate amount.)

10. Do you have a Safe Deposit Box at a bank? ❏ Yes ❏ No
    - a. Minimum value of contents: $ _____
    - b. Maximum value of contents: $ _____
    - c. Does any one employee have the authority to access the Safe Deposit Box alone?
      ❏ Yes ❏ No (If "Yes," please attach an explanation, including the identity of the person and the position.)

11. Do you require employees who handle money, securities, books, and records to take a two-week vacation each year? ❏ Yes ❏ No

Other Control Comments:

Loss Information:

Please provide the following information for *__all__* loss(es) discovered during the past five (5) years (whether reimbursed or not) that involve, or potentially involve, perils of the type covered by the policy.

Exhibit 8.1   Continued

Cause of Loss	Date Discovered	Gross Amount of Loss (Actual or Estimated)	Amount Received from Insurance Less Salvage	Deductible at Time of Loss	Location, If Other Than Main Office

Notice: Any person who knowingly and with intent to defraud any insurance company or other person files an application for insurance containing any materially false information, or conceals for the purpose of misleading, information concerning any fact material thereto commits a fraudulent insurance act, which is a crime. (In New York, such crime is subject to a civil penalty not to exceed five thousand dollars and the stated value of the claim for each violation.)

Signed by:_____   Dated:_____

Title:_____

Please attach the following supporting documentation when submitting this application:

Annual Report and 10k
Audited Financial Statement
CPA Management Letter and Management's Response Thereto

Samuel Y. Fisher, Jr., ARM, CPCU
2002 - S. Fisher & Associates, LLC
All Rights Reserved

Source: Samuel Y. Fisher, Jr., ARM, CPCU © 2002, S. Fisher & Associates, LLC. All rights reserved. Reprinted with permission.

Review of Contractual Risk Allocation

Chapters 3, 4, and 5 discuss how risk is allocated in U.C.C. Articles 3, 4, and 4A with respect to checks and wire transfers, and Chapter 6 discusses the rules for ACH transfers. The Company will have entered into agreements with its bank for the provision by the bank of wire transfer and ACH services. A detailed discussion of the negotiation of these agreements with the bank is beyond the scope of this book.

We have observed, however, and it is of great importance to note in the context of risk management, that *the standard form of bank agreement often varies the statutory allocation of risk.* For example, a provision that exculpates the bank from liability "except to the extent that the Bank's conduct shall have constituted gross negligence or willful misconduct" would significantly vary the liability of the bank for fraudulent checks and for fraudulent or erroneous funds transfers.

Short-period reporting requirements also indirectly vary the liability of the bank. Within the context of risk management, the importance of prompt reconciliation of bank statements has been emphasized. It may appear reasonable for a company to agree to report fraudulent or erroneous transfers shortly after the receipt of its bank statements. A company should be wary, however, of a provision that states, "Customer shall notify Bank within ___ days after receipt of the periodic statement" of an alleged fraudulent or erroneous item. That kind of provision may impose significant liability on the company that would otherwise have been imposed on the bank by law.

It is one thing for company management knowingly to agree to assume liability greater than that imposed by law, but quite another thing for the company to assume such liability in ignorance of how the liability is allocated by statute. Management must, of course, rely on counsel. Yet even very competent counsel is often unfamiliar with payment system law. Perhaps it would not be unduly audacious for treasury personnel to suggest to counsel that this book or similar reading might be a useful addition to the law library.

MANAGING PAYMENT SYSTEMS DISRUPTIONS

Backup files and off-site storage are important to a reliable plan for the management of corporate payment systems risks attributable to payment systems disruptions. Updating of the backup files and the regular transfer of records to off-site storage should be documented. Periodic testing to confirm that the procedures are followed and workable should be overseen by senior management. After the September 11, 2001, attack on the United States and the resulting disruptions in the New York City financial center, the Association for Finance Professionals (AFP) published a checklist for its membership,[1] paraphrased as follows:

Contacts

- Maintain a current list of bank contacts and store at a backup site and on handheld computers or personal digital assistants (PDAs). Keep printouts at off-site locations and at the home of key treasury personnel.
- Image important documents and store two copies at two different off-site locations.
- Maintain a list of key employees, with home and cell telephone numbers, and ensure that they have the list at their homes and on PDAs.
- Cross-train employees for emergency work at different physical locations.

Payments Applications

- Encourage direct deposit of payroll.
- Promote electronic bill payment.
- Evaluate impact on the company of delays in cash receipts.
- Plan liquidity—how to manage if commercial paper cannot be settled or sold. Are credit lines available if not ordinarily used? Can global liquidity play a role?

Communications

- What happens if the telephone lines go down at the company? At the bank(s)?
- Establish backup location(s) for the company's funds-transfer system. Maintain a consolidated list of user names and passwords and be sure the bank has call-back verification procedures.
- Arrange key employee home access for treasury workstation and electronic banking systems with back-up authorization and approval procedures.
- Arrange with banks for backup for payroll and other critical funds transfers.

- Arrange backup transmission for payroll, lockbox, payables, and receivables files.
- Arrange alternative check printing locations.
- Review sources for information about disaster planning and outsourcing alternatives.

The authors suggest that the management of risks to corporate payment systems in disaster mode be periodically reviewed so that special requirements are not overlooked.

The following checklists, extracted from the chapters of this book, can guide a thorough risk management assessment and documentation of procedures. The discussion in each chapter provides an explanation of the risks and the mitigation opportunities.

MANAGING CHECK PAYMENT SYSTEM RISKS

Chapter 3 contains a detailed discussion of the topics in this risk management checklist.

Company That Issues Checks

The issuer should plan and document dual controls for all aspects of issuing checks, from inception through the process of reconciling bank statements.

- *Approved vendors.* Control should be established for the approval of new vendors to the company.
- *Payment approvals.* Before checks are issued, the invoices or other written requests for payment should be approved by a process independent of the signatory to the check.
- *Check writing.* The check stock removed from storage for check writing should be logged, and void checks should be logged as well.
- *Check signing.* The signature process may be automated under dual controls.
- *Bank controls.* The drawer can mitigate risks of unauthorized, high-dollar withdrawal transactions (whether by check, wire, or ACH) through controls at its bank.

- *Timely review of bank statements.* The issuer of checks should timely review and reconcile its bank statements.
- *Check stock log.* A log document should record beginning and ending check numbers of check stock as ordered and received.
- *Controlled access storage and record of checks used.* The company should create continuously locked storage for the check stock with dual access controls.
- *Control of ordering checks.* The company management should determine who is authorized to order checks and to whose attention checks are delivered for entry into the controlled access storage.
- *Check stock.* Elaborate check stock security features are available through check stock printing companies.
- *Positive pay arrangements.* An agreement with the company's bank for the provision of positive pay services is an extremely effective way to prevent certain types of fraud. It is important to note, however, that a typical positive pay arrangement does not detect all types of check fraud.

Company That Receives Checks

A number of businesses receive checks by mail, and many businesses receive many checks at the point of sale (POS).

Retail POS risk procedures require an assessment of the degree of risk that the company is willing to accept.

- *Verify identity.* Most retailers verify the identity of the person who is the drawer of the check with the information preprinted on the check.
- *Verify MICR stripe appearance.* Training those who accept POS checks to review the appearance of the magnetic ink character recognition (MICR) line on the check helps deter the acceptance of forged checks.

- *Third-party checks.* Knowledge of the potential problems in regard to "holder in due course" will facilitate an understanding of why retailers rarely accept third-party checks.

General business receipts are receipts outside the retail POS environment.

- *Large payments not made by wire transfer.* A business expecting very large payments to be made by check, instead of by wire, may request payment by "certified check," or official bank checks sometimes called "bank drafts," "cashier's checks," or "teller's checks."
- *Ensure that the checks received are all deposited to the company's account.* Lockbox processing by a bank provides another method for this control.
- *Reviewing accounts receivable and "past due" accounts helps catch theft and improves cash flow as well.*
- *Reconcile reports of change in accounts receivable to the total of bank deposits.*

MANAGING WIRE TRANSFER PAYMENT SYSTEM RISKS

Chapters 4 and 5 contain detailed discussions of the topics in this risk management checklist.

Important: The risks of a funds-transfer payment system are best controlled before a wire transfer order is released by the company to its bank. Preventing errors and fraud is very difficult thereafter.

Originator and Its Bank

A company should have a written agreement with its bank for the bank to accept and execute the company's wire transfer payment orders.

The agreement should not allow the bank to shift its legal liabilities back to the company by short-period reporting requirements. For example, a company should be wary of a provision that states, "Customer shall notify Bank within ___ days after receipt of the periodic statement" of an alleged fraudulent or erroneous item. See Chapter 4 about this very high priority for managing corporate wire transfer payment system risk.

- The personnel of the company responsible for sending wire transfers should carefully double-check the wire transfer amounts and instructions before sending a wire.
- Establish procedures consistent with the bank's written agreement if a payment order is canceled or amended.
- Dual control review of nonrecurring wire transfer instructions.
- For recurring wire transfers, preformatted wire transfer orders and dual review of variable input of transaction amounts.
- Use the bank's reporting services to verify that payment orders have been executed.
- Promptly review and verify with the company's records all bank notices and bank statements.
- Keep current records of the name of the responsible persons in departments at the bank to whom notices of errors or problems should be addressed.

Foreign payments: A company's personnel should not try to reinvent the wheel; they should rely on its bank's guidance and expertise for the payment systems appropriate to the locations, currencies, frequency, and amounts required.

Sending and Receiving Banks

The originator should carefully consider the risk of specifying intermediary banks for its wire transfer payment orders.

MANAGING ACH PAYMENT SYSTEM RISKS

In managing ACH payment system risks, the issues are generally similar to those associated with computer processing of checks and electronic terminal processing of outgoing wire transfers. In general, the methods of controlling electronic funds transfers should also be applied to ACH transactions.

- Train accounting and treasury personnel to have a clear understanding of the ACH Rules and any notices or reports the company may receive, either as an Originator or a Receiver.
- Establish a daily reconciliation procedure, and be prepared to notify the company's ODFI or RDFI of any errors or questions. Never miss the time deadlines of the ACH Rules. Management should review to see that the daily procedures are being followed.
- Plan continuing controls for the risks of electronic origination of entries to receive funds and the timely and accurate accounting for receipt of those funds.
- Establish internal controls for authorizing the receipt of funds by ACH processing. Customer account records need to be noted for ACH processing.
- Make certain that prior written authorization is obtained for withdrawals from consumer accounts.
- Establish dollar limits for transactions to be processed and for warning messages.

Important: A business using ACH payment systems should modify its internal procedures to synchronize with its financial institution's deadlines under the ACH Rules.

Unwavering maintenance of legal rights and continuing attention to internal controls, checklists, and procedures, and promptly initiating written inquiries about any questions or problems, are key to effective management of corporate payment systems risks.

ENDNOTE

1. AFP Payments Advisory Group, "In the Aftermath: Guarding Against Payments Disruptions," *AFP Update* Vol. 22, No. 1 (December 2001/January 2002): 4. This is sent to members only.

Glossary

ACH or Automated Clearing House System   A funds-transfer system for the clearing of paperless interbank transfers created as an alternative to the check system. Approximately 35 regional ACH associations are members of the National Automated Clearing House Association (NACHA). The system clears electronic entries pursuant to the NACHA Rules. An ACH Operator provides clearing, settlement, and delivery services for the ACH entries. The Federal Reserve Banks act as the ACH Operators in each of the Federal Reserve Districts; in some districts, private sector entities may also act as the ACH Operators under an agreement with NACHA.

American Bankers Association (ABA)   The trade association of American bankers. The ABA is authorized to assign routing and transit identification numbers.

Association for Financial Professionals (AFP)   The trade association of corporate treasury executives, the corporate counterpart of the ABA.

Authorized account An account of a bank customer that is designated by the customer as a source from which payment orders for funds transfers under U.C.C. Article 4A, sent to the bank by the customer and executed by the bank, may be reimbursed to the bank.

Batch A group of transactions that occur during a given time interval. Batches of transaction data may be contained in a computer file for transmission or processing (compare with real-time or on-line). In the ACH system, a batch of entries constitutes a single unit for processing purposes.

Book transfer An electronic funds transfer in which the originator and the beneficiary use the same bank. The bank debits the account of the originator and credits the account of the beneficiary. See *On-us transaction.*

Cardholder certificate An electronic record created to authenticate a cardholder or party to an electronic commerce transaction.

CCD Cash concentration or disbursement entries in ACH transactions. Such an entry allows a corporate user to concentrate cash in a single, typically interest-bearing account and to disburse cash as needed to other accounts maintained by the user and its affiliates.

Check guarantee or check verification service A company or system offering merchants insurance against bad check losses by guaranteeing payment of a check or by verifying the authenticity of the check or its presenter.

Check reader A device that reads the MICR on checks.

Clearing The process of collecting checks or electronic payment entries from the drawee bank.

Clearing House Interbank Payment System (CHIPS) The funds-transfer system owned and operated by the New York Clearing House Association for large-dollar transfers.

Commercial cards Plastic debit or credit cards for businesses (vs. consumer cards), including corporate cards, business cards, and purchase cards. Corporate cards are issued to the employees of a corporation, but the company is liable for charges to the cards and the cards have separate card numbers. Purchase cards are issued to companies with a variety of limits; for example, the company can control daily and monthly spending limits and where the cards can be used; all cards have the same account number. A business card is similar to a corporate card, but each employee is financially responsible for the purchases and the company reimburses employees for verified business purchases.

Correspondent bank A bank that maintains an account with another bank for the acceptance of deposits, the settlement of transactions, and, typically, the exchange of other services with the other bank.

Counterfeit device or check A card or other device that is printed, embossed, or encoded but has not been authorized for issuance by the purported issuer. Alternately, a card or other device that the issuer has authorized but that has subsequently been altered without the issuer's authorization. With respect to checks, the term usually denotes a check that has been manufactured by a perpetrator of fraud that is intended to imitate a genuine check of the victim of the fraud.

CTX A corporate trade exchange entry is initiated for the purpose of transferring funds from one organization to another, along with electronic data regarding the payment in connection with the transaction, in an ACH transaction.

Daylight overdraft   A debit balance in the customer's account that occurs in the course of the banking day and is expected to be repaid by a credit to the account prior to the end of the banking day.

Debit card   A card that can debit the cardholder's cash account.

Dedicated line   (Also called a *leased line* or *private line.*) A communications circuit between two end points that is permanently connected.

Depository Financial Institution (DFI)   A financial institution participating in an ACH transaction.

Device driver   A module of software enabling use of a specific hardware device, such as a modem, a printer, or a card reader.

Draft caption   See *Electronic draft capture.*

Edge Act Corporation   Chartered by the Federal Reserve to engage in international banking operations. The Federal Reserve Board acts on applications by United States and foreign banking organizations to establish Edge corporations.

Electronic benefits transfer (EBT) card   This card may have a magnetic stripe or a small microprocessor on it. The card is used to replace the paper distributed by the government for programs like the Women, Infants, and Children program and food stamps. Cardholders may use these cards and have the charges deducted from their available benefit dollars for the programs in which they are participating. These cards are increasing in popularity and use throughout the United States.

Electronic commerce   Also "e-commerce." The purchase and sale of goods or services over the Internet or through proprietary intranets.

Electronic draft capture (EDC)   Now a term used to describe electronic communications to process from the holder to the drawee the drafts representing credit card or other electronic transactions for settlement.

Electronic funds transfer (EFT)   Generally, the paperless transfer of funds between accounts at depository financial institutions. Wholesale funds transfers between business entities are covered by U.C.C. Article 4A. Transfers of funds into or out of a consumer's account are covered by the Electronic Fund Transfer Act and by Regulation E of the Federal Reserve Board. Under U.C.C. Article 4A, a funds transfer may be initiated by instructions transmitted orally or in writing, as well as electronically. The terms *EFT, funds transfer,* and *wire transfer* are often used interchangeably. An electronic funds transfer system (EFTS) is an electronic communications system to transfer funds from a payor to a payee or to transmit financial data. Examples of EFTSs are ACH, Fedwire, CHIPS, and SWIFT.

Federal funds rate   Purchases and sales in the open market of U.S. Treasury and federal agency securities are the Federal Reserve's principal tool for implementing monetary policy. The short-term objective for open market operations is specified by the Federal Open Market Committee (FOMC). This objective can be a desired quantity of reserves or a desired price (the federal funds rate). The federal funds rate is the interest rate at which depository institutions lend balances at the Federal Reserve to other depository institutions overnight.

Field   The smallest defined data element within an electronic file. A series of fields are a record and a group of records are a file.

Hologram   A three-dimensional image created by a laser. Holograms are used to make counterfeiting more difficult—for example, in regard to plastic cards.

International Organization for Standardization   The organization providing industry standards ("ISO standards") for financial transactions and telecommunications messages.

Magnetic ink character recognition (MICR)   The MICR characters on a check are printed in special ink. An MICR-encoded check passes through magnetic heads in a reader/sorter to be magnetized and then read.

Magnetic stripe   A stripe of magnetic information affixed to the back of a plastic credit or debit card. The stripe contains the customer and account information required to complete electronic financial transactions. The physical and magnetic characteristics of this stripe are specified in ISO standards. A magnetic stripe "card" reader reads information from the magnetic stripe and transmits that information to a computer processor.

Merchant depository account   A demand deposit account established by a merchant with a bank to receive payment for sales drafts submitted to the bank card plan.

Misdescription   A misdescription is simply an erroneous description, but in an electronic funds transfer under U.C.C. Article 4A, is more narrowly said to occur when the sender of a payment order uses both a name and a number to describe either the beneficiary or a bank in the funds transfer. The misdescription results because the name and number identify different entities. Either the name or the number is erroneous.

ODFI, or originating depository financial institution   An ODFI is an ACH Participating Depository Financial Institution (PDFI) with respect to entries it receives from the Originator and transmits to the ACH Operator for transmission to the RDFI for the Receivers' account. An entry that deposits funds into the Receiver's account is a credit entry, and one that pulls funds from the Receiver's account is a debit entry.

On-line financial transaction   A financial transaction that is settled in a single on-line message (vs. batch processing).

On-us transaction   A transaction in which the payor and payee utilize the same bank. In a check on-us transaction, the drawer draws the check on the same bank that the payee uses to deposit the check. In an electronic funds transfer, the originator and the beneficiary use the same bank. On-us electronic transactions are also known as "book transfers."

Paper draft   Sales slips, credit slips, cash disbursement slips, drafts, vouchers, and other documents indicating a drawer's requesting a drawee to pay a holder. For example, a draft, document or electronic, for a credit card charge.

Participating depository financial institution (participating DFI)
A financial institution authorized to participate in an ACH. See also *ODFI* and *RDFI.*

Payment order   An instruction by a sender in a U.C.C. Article 4A funds transfer to a receiving bank to make a payment. A funds transfer is a chain of payment orders. The first payment order in a funds-transfer chain is from the originator to the originator's bank, and the last payment order is from a bank in the chain to the beneficiary's bank.

Personal identification number (PIN)   A numeric code for an individual to be identified to a computer system, whether as an individual (as a consumer) or on behalf of a business (as an authorized person). PINs are issued and maintained under various security systems. An individual PIN is linked to the primary account number for that PIN.

Point of sale (POS)   ACH terminology distinguishes between POS and POP. In **point-of-sale (POS)** ACH transfers, debit cards, credit cards, or a merchants card or device are used to pay the merchant for goods or services. In **point-of-purchase (POP)** ACH transfers, consumers' checks become "electronic checks," that is, checks that are converted into ACH debit entries to pay for goods or services at the point of purchase.

Presentment   The presentation by a collecting bank to the drawee bank of a check for payment.

RDFI, or receiving depository financial institution   An RDFI is an ACH Participating DFI with respect to entries it receives from the ACH Operator for the Receivers' accounts.

Regulation E   Authorized by the 1978 Electronic Funds Transfer Act (EFTA), the board of governors of the Federal Reserve System issued Regulation E, and authorizes staff interpretations of the regulation, to protect consumers. Regulation E applies to an electronic funds transfer authorizing a financial institution to debit or credit a consumer's account, a consumer's account being an account established primarily for personal, family, or household purposes.

Sales draft   A record that a drawer cardholder has authorized a provider of goods or services to obtain funds from its account with a drawee for the purchase of goods or services.

Security procedure   A procedure agreed upon by a bank and a customer to verify that a U.C.C. Article 4A payment order purporting to have been sent by the customer is actually that of the customer. Also a procedure to detect errors in the customer's transmission of payment orders.

Settlement   Payment between banks for cleared payment instructions or checks. Also the reporting of settlement amounts owed by one member to another, or to a card-issuing concern, as a result of clearing. This is the actual buying and selling for transactions between the merchants, processors, and acquirers, along with the card-issuing entities.

Smart card   A credit or debit card embodying a computer chip with memory and interactive capabilities used for identification and to store additional data about the cardholder, cardholder account, or both. Also called an *integrated circuit card* or a *chip card.*

Stored value card   A card on which "electronic funds" are loaded for the payment of goods and services at the point of sale. The value stored on the card is decreased with each purchase.

SWIFT, Society for Worldwide International Financial Communications   An international telecommunications network for the sending of payments and other messages.

Terminal   A device enabling the user to communicate with a computer. The device is sometimes called an *input/output device* or an *I/O terminal.*

Wholesale funds transfer   The term is not a precise one and is not authoritatively defined anywhere. A transfer involving a consumer, which would normally be governed by Regulation E, would not be a wholesale funds transfer. A transfer utilizing either of the two large-dollar value funds transfer systems, Fedwire and CHIPS, would typically be a wholesale funds transfer. A U.C.C. Article 4A funds transfer of a large-dollar amount not involving a consumer, but also not involving a large-value funds transfer system, may also be called a wholesale funds transfer. Small-value funds transfers are called "retail" wire transfers.

Wire transfer transaction   A term commonly applied to an electronic funds transfer transaction. See *Electronic funds transfer.*

References

PRINTED PUBLICATIONS

AFP Update. Contact Association for Finance Professionals for membership.

Friedman, Milton. *Money Mischief: Episodes in Monetary History.* San Diego, CA: Harcourt Trade Publishers, 1994.

Geva, Benjamin (with contributions by S. A. Heller, P. S. Turner, and S. R. Vicksman). *The Law of Electronic Funds Transfers.* Newark, NJ: Matthew Bender, 1992 (revised annually).

Patrikis, Ernest T. (with Thomas C. Baxter Jr. and Raj K. Bhala). *Wire Transfers: A Guide to U.S. and International Laws Governing Funds Transfers.* Rolling Meadow, IL: Bankers Publishing Co., 1993.

Turner, Paul S. *Law of Payment Systems and EFT.* New York: Aspen Law and Business, 1999 (revised annually). *Note:* This annually updated book includes Mr. Turner's most recent text on *Negotiating Wire Transfer Agreements.* (See below.)

References

Turner, Paul S. *Negotiating Wire Transfer Agreements: A Guide for Treasury Executives, Bankers, and Attorneys.* Bethesda, MD: Treasury Management Association (now Association for Finance Professionals), 1996.

Subcommittee on Payments, Uniform Commercial Code Committee. *Model Positive Pay Services Agreement and Commentary.* Chicago, IL: American Bar Association, 1999.

Working Group on Electronic Financial Services, Subcommittee on Electronic Commercial Practices, Uniform Commercial Code Committee. *Model Funds Transfer Services Agreement and Commentary.* Chicago, IL: American Bar Association, 1994.

OTHER REFERENCE RESOURCES

Association for Finance Professionals; reference books; *www.afponline.org.*

Federal Reserve Bank, Discount Window. *Payment Systems Risk, Frequently Asked Questions. www.frbdiscountwindow.org/psrfaq.htm.*

www.newyorkfed.org/banking/information. A good general reference about banking systems.

www.nych.org. Web site for the New York Clearing House.

www.SWIFT.com. Current information about SWIFT services and initiatives.

Index

A

Index

Index

Index

Index

Index